The Little Book
of

NAUGHTY
LIMERICKS

The Little Book
of

NAUGHTY
LIMERICKS

~•~

Edited by
TOM KEEGAN

p

This is a Parragon Book
This edition published in 2005

Parragon
Queen Street House
4 Queen Street
Bath BA1 1HE, UK

Produced by Magpie Books, an imprint of
Robinson Publishing Ltd, London

Copyright © Parragon 1998

Cover image courtesy of Getty Images
Cover by Talking Design

ISBN 1-40546-127-6

A copy of the British Library Cateloguing-in-Publication Data
is available from the British Library

Printed in China

Contents

~·≀≀·~

Introduction   6

1. LIMERICKS BY LEAR   9

2. THERE ONCE WAS A MAN …   40

3. MY MOTHER CAME FROM
HUNSTANTON   79

4. NAUGHTY LIMERICKS   110

5. VERY NAUGHTY
LIMERICKS   149

6. JOLLY FUNNY LIMERICKS   176

7. THE FUNNIEST LIMERICKS
EVER   208

8. A LIMERICK LUCKY DIP   236

Introduction

~❦~

Collecting the material for this book was hard enough, but writing limericks, that's another thing altogether! It needs an inventive mind to come up with good limericks. Not only do the first, second and fifth lines have to rhyme (as do the third and fourth), but each line must have the right number of syllables and the limerick has to make sense, have a point and be funny. Managing all that takes a considerable amount of mental dexterity.

If you feel like writing your own limericks, try not to start with "There was an old man from ..." or some such beginning. It tends to become rather dull as you always end up writing about old men from Nuneaton, not to mention the problem that rhymes about Nuneaton are hard to come by. Except "eaten" of course, and "lambs bleating" (well nearly) ... oh well, you get the idea.

Thankfully some very clever and funny people have taken the time and trouble to produce the witty limericks included in this collection, so sit back and enjoy the wit, wisdom, cheek and sometimes downright naughtiness of The Little Book of Ribald Rhymes.

Chapter 1

LIMERICKS BY LEAR

Edward Lear is rightly thought to be the father of the limerick. Lear was not the first to write limericks, but it was he who made them popular. His limericks, like much of his nonsense verse, were written for the children of the Earl of Derby, for whom Lear worked as an artist between 1846 and 1895.

Lear's version of the limerick often repeats the opening line as the punchline. This may seem repetitive when compared to later limericks, but Lear introduced a whole new range of poetic images, and his illustrations complemented his rhymes perfectly.

There was a young person in pink
Who called out for something to drink.
But they said, "Oh my daughter,
There's nothing but water!"
Which vexed that young person in pink.

There was an old person of Florence
Who held mutton chops in abhorrence.
He purchased a bustard
And fried him in mustard,
Which choked that old person of Florence.

There was an old person of Loo
Who said, "What on earth shall I do?"
When they said "Go away!"
She continued to stay,
That vexatious old person of Loo.

There was an old person of Sheen
Whose expression was calm and serene.
He sat in the water
And drank bottled porter,
That placid old person of Sheen.

There was an old man of Spithead
Who opened the window and said,
"Fil-jomble fil-jumble,
Fil-rumble-come-tumble!"
That doubtful old man of Spithead.

There was an old person of Brig
Who purchased no end of a wig.
So that only his nose
And the end of his toes,
Could be seen when he walked about Brig.

There was an old person of Deal
Who in walking used only his heel.
When they said, "Tell us why?"
He made no reply
That mysterious person of Deal.

There was an old person of Crowle
Who lived in the nest of an owl.
When they screamed in the nest
He screamed out with the rest,
That depressing old person of Crowle.

There was an old person of Sestri
Who sat himself down in the vestry.
When they said, "You are wrong!"
He merely said, "Bong!"
That repulsive old person of Sestri.

There was an old person in Rey
Whose feelings were tinged with dismay.
She purchased two parrots
And fed them with carrots,
Which pleased that old person in grey.

～｛▲｝～

There was an old person of Bow,
Whom nobody happened to know,
So they gave him some soap
And said coldly, "We hope
You will go back directly to Bow."

～｛▲｝～

There was an old person of Bude
Whose deportment was vicious and crude.
He wore a large ruff
Of pale straw-coloured stuff
Which perplexed all the people of Bude.

There was an old man in a tree
Whose whiskers were lovely to see.
But the birds of the air
Pluck'd them perfectly bare,
To make themselves nests in that tree.

There was a young lady of Corsica
Who purchased a little brown saucy-cur.
Which she fed upon ham
And hot raspberry jam,
That expensive young lady of Corsica.

There was an old person of Skye
Who waltzed with a bluebottle fly
They buzz'd a sweet tune
To the light of the moon
And entranced all the people of Skye.

There was an old man of Dunblane
Who greatly resembled a crane.
But they said, "Is it wrong,
Since your legs are so long,
To request you won't stay in Dunblane?"

There was an old person of Ware
Who rode on the back of a bear.
When asked, "Does it trot?"
He said, "Certainly not!
He's a mopsikon floppsikon bear!"

There was an old man of Dumbree
Who taught little owls to drink tea.
For he said, "To eat mice
Is not proper or nice,"
That amiable man of Dumbree.

There was an old person of Shoreham
Whose habits were marked by decorum.
He brought an umbrella
And sat in the cellar,
Which pleased all the people of Shoreham.

There was an old person of Wilts
Who constantly walked upon stilts.
He wreathed them with lilies
And daffy-down-dillies,
That elegant person of Wilts.

There was an old person whose remorse
Induced him to drink caper sauce.
For they said, "If mixed up
With some old claret cup,
It will certainly soothe your remorse."

There was an old person of Filey
Of whom his acquaintance spoke highly.
He danced perfectly well,
To the sound of a bell
And delighted the people of Filey.

There was an old man of El Hums
Who lived upon nothing but crumbs.
Which he picked off the ground
With the other birds around
In the roads and the lanes of El Hums.

There was an old man of Messina
Whose daughter was named Opsibeena.
She wore a small wig
And rode out on a pig,
To the perfect delight of Messina.

There was a young lady whose nose
Continually prospers and grows.
When it grew out of sight
She exclaimed in a fright,
"Oh! Farewell to the end of my nose!"

There was an old lady of Winchelsea,
Who said, "If you needle or pin shall see
On the floor of my room
Sweep it up with the broom!"
That exhaustive old lady of Winchelsea.

There was an old man, who when little
Fell casually into a kettle.
But, growing too stout
He could never get out,
So he passes all his life in that kettle.

There was a young lady in white
Who looked out at the depths of the night.
But the birds of the air
Filled her heart with despair,
And oppressed that young lady in white.

There was an old person in Putney
Whose food was roast spiders and chutney
Which he took with his tea,
Within sight of the sea,
That romantic old person in Putney.

There was an old man on whose nose
Most birds in the air could repose.
But they all flew away
At the closing of the day,
Which relieved that old man and his nose.

There was a young lady of Clare
Who was sadly pursued by a bear.
When she found she was tired
She abruptly expired
That unfortunate lady of Clare.

There was a young lady of Parma
Whose conduct grew calmer and calmer.
When they said "Are you dumb?"
She merely said "Hum!"
That provoking young lady of Parma.

There was an old man who said "How
Shall I flee from that horrible cow?
I will sit on the stile,
And continue to smile,
Which may soften the heart of that cow."

There was an old man of Aosta,
Who possessed a large cow but he lost her.
But they said, "Don't you see,
She has rushed up a tree?
You invidious old man of Aosta."

There was an old person of Ems
Who casually fell in the Thames.
And when he was found,
They said he was drowned,
That unlucky old person of Ems.

There was an old person of Ewell
Who chiefly subsisted on gruel.
But to make it more nice,
He inserted some mice
Which refreshed that old person of Ewell.

There was an old lady of Prague
Whose language was horribly vague.
When they said, "Are these caps?"
She answered, "Perhaps!"
That oracular lady of Prague.

There was an old person of Sparta
Who had twenty five sons and one "darter."
He fed them on snails
And weighed them in scales,
That wonderful person of Sparta.

There was an old person of Gretna
Who rushed to the crater of Etna.
When they said, "Is it hot?"
He replied, "No it is not,"
That mendacious old person of Gretna.

There was a young lady of Sweden
Who went by the slow train to Weedon.
When they cried, "Weedon Station!"
She made no observation
But thought she should go back to Sweden.

There was an old man of the Cape
Who possessed a large Barbary ape.
Till the ape one dark night
Set the house all alight,
Which burned that old man of the Cape.

There was a young girl of Majorca
Whose aunt was a very fast walker.
She walked seventy miles
And leaped fifteen stiles,
Which astonished that girl of Majorca.

There was a young lady of Welling
Whose praise all the world was a telling.
She played on a harp
And caught several carp,
That accomplished young lady of Welling.

There was an old person of Tartary
Who divided his jugular artery.
But he screeched to his wife,
And she said, "Oh my life!
Your death will be felt by all Tartary."

There was an old person of Spain
Who hated all trouble and pain.
So he sat on a chair
With his feet in the air,
That umbrageous old person of Spain.

There was an old man of the coast
Who placidly sat on a post.
But when it was cold
He relinquished his hold
And called for some hot buttered toast.

There was an old man of Berlin
Whose form was uncommonly thin.
Till he once by mistake
Was mixed up in a cake,
So they baked that old man of Berlin.

There was a young lady of Tyre
Who swept the loud chords of a lyre.
At the sound of each sweep
She enraptured the deep
And enchanted the city of Tyre.

There was an old person of Bangor
Whose face was distorted with anger!
He tore off his boots
And subsisted on roots,
That irascible person of Bangor.

There was an old man who said, "Hush!
I perceive a young bird in the bush!"
When they said, "Is is small?"
He replied, "Not at all!
It is four times as big as the bush."

There was an old man in a pew
Whose waistcoat was spotted with blue.
But he tore it to pieces
To give to his nieces,
That cheerful old man in a pew.

There was an old person of Troy
Whose drink was warm brandy and soy,
    Which he took with a spoon
    By the light of the moon
In sight of the city of Troy.

There was an old person of Cromer
Who stood on one leg to read Homer.
    When he found he grew stiff
    He jumped over a cliff,
Which concluded that person of Cromer.

There was an old person of Rheims
Who was troubled with horrible dreams.
    So, to keep him awake
    They fed him with cake,
Which amused that old person of Rheims.

There was an old man of the Nile,
Who sharpened his nails with a file,
Till he cut off his thumbs,
And said calmly, "This comes
Of sharpening one's nails with a file!"

There was an old lady whose folly
Induced her to sit in a holly.
Whereupon by a thorn
Her dress being torn,
She quickly became melancholy.

There was an old man of Nepal,
From his horse had a terrible fall.
But, though split quite in two,
With some very strong glue
They mended that man of Nepal.

There was an old man of th' Abruzzi
So blind that he couldn't his foot see.
When they said, "That's your toe!"
He replied, "Is it so?"
That doubtful old man of Abruzzi.

~ 🐝 ~

There was an old man of Apulia
Whose conduct was very peculiar.
He fed twenty sons,
Upon nothing but buns
That whimsical man of Apulia.

~ 🐝 ~

There was an old man with a poker,
Who painted his face with red ochre,
When they said, "You're a guy!"
He made no reply,
But knocked them all down with his poker.

There was a young lady whose nose
Was so long that it reached to her toes.
She hired an old lady
Whose conduct was steady
To carry that wonderful nose.

There was a young lady of Turkey
Who wept when the weather was murky.
When the day turned out fine
She ceased to repine
That capricious young lady of Turkey.

There was an old person whose habits
Induced him to feed upon rabbits.
When he'd eaten eighteen
He turned perfectly green,
Upon which he relinquished those habits.

There was an old person of Dover
Who rushed through a field of blue clover,
But some very large bees
Stung his nose and his knees
So he very soon went back to Dover.

There was an old man of the Wrekin
Whose shoes made a horrible creaking.
But they said, "Tell us whether
Your shoes are of leather,
Or of what, you old man of the Wrekin?"

There was a young lady of Ryde
Whose shoe strings were seldom untied.
She purchased some clogs
And some small spotted dogs,
And frequently walked about Ryde.

There was an old lady of Chertsey
Who made a remarkable curtsy.
She twirled round and round,
Till she sank underground
Which distressed all the people of Chertsey.

There was an old man of the Dee
Who was sadly annoyed by a flea.
When he said, "I will scratch it,"
They gave him a hatchet,
Which grieved that old man of the Dee.

There was an old man of Vienna
Who lived upon tincture of senna.
When that did not agree
He took camomile tea,
That nasty old man of Vienna.

There was a young lady whose eyes
Were unique as to colour and size.
When she opened them wide
People all turned aside
And started away in surprise.

There was an old person of Dean
Who dined on one pea and one bean.
For he said, "More than that
Would make me too fat,"
That cautious old person of Dean.

There was a young person whose history
Was always considered a mystery.
She sat in a ditch,
Although no one knew which
And composed a small treatise on history.

There was an old man of Cape Horn
Who wished he had never been born.
So he sat on a chair
Till he died of despair,
That dolorous old man of Cape Horn.

The next one is not by Lear but inspired by him . . .

There was a young man of Cape Horn
Who wished he'd never been born,
And he wouldn't have been
If his father had seen
That the end of the rubber was torn.

There was an old man of Dundee
Who frequented the top of a tree.
When disturbed by the crows
He abruptly arose
And exclaimed, "I'll return to Dundee."

As before, not by Lear but a version of the previous limerick.

There was an old man of Dundee
Who molested an ape in a tree.
The result was most horrid
All bum and no forehead
Three arms and a purple goatee.

There was a young lady of Norway
Who casually sat in a doorway.
When the door squeezed her flat,
She exclaimed, "What was that?"
This courageous young lady of Norway.

There was a young lady of Greenwich
Whose garments were bordered with spinach.
But a large spotty calf
Bit her shawl quite in half,
Which alarmed that young lady of Greenwich.

There was an old man in a tree
Who was horribly bored by a bee.
When they said, "Does it buzz?"
He replied, "Yes it does!
It's a regular brute of a bee."

The smile on the famed Mona Lisa
Has long been a bit of a teaser.
Perhaps Leonardo
In a fit of bravado
Made as if he were going to squeeze her.

With his last dying breath cried the ocelot
"Being wrapped in these coils hurts an offalot.
I've made a mistake
In judging this snake,
I'd thought the boas to be a docile lot."

There was an old woman of Gloucester
Whose parrot two guineas it cost her.
But his tongue never ceasing
Was vastly displeasing
To that talkative woman of Gloucester.

There was as old person of Hurst
Who drank when he was a thirst.
When they said, "You'll grow fatter!"
He answered, "No matter!"
That globular old person of Hurst.

There was an old man who supposed
That the street door was partially closed.
But some very large rats
Ate his coat and his hats
While that futile old gentleman dozed.

There was an old man who said, "Hush!
I perceive a young bird in this bush!"
When they said, "Is it small?"
He replied, "Not at all!
It is four times as big as the bush."

There was an old man of Thermopylae
Who never did anything properly.
But they said, "If you choose
To boil eggs in your shoes
You shall never remain in Thermopylae."

There was an old man who said, "Well!
Will nobody answer that bell?
I have pulled day and night
Till my hair has turned white
But nobody answers that bell."

There was an old man of St Bees
Who was horribly stung by a wasp.
When they said, "Does it hurt?"
He replied, "No it doesn't –
It's a good job it wasn't a hornet!"

Chapter 2

THERE ONCE WAS A MAN …

This is a chapter of general limericks. Those who know anything about limericks may have noticed that the vast majority of them contain rude words. This one sums up the tone of most others:

> *There once was an anthologist who*
> *Decided that nothing's taboo.*
> *His words are so rude*
> *His verses so lewd*
> *I'm sure they'll appeal to you.*

But have no fear! The content of this chapter, though sometimes suggestive, should not cause too many uncomfortable moments.

There was an old he-wolf called Gambart
Beware of him if thou a lamb art.
Else thy tail and thy toes
And thy innocent nose
Will be ground by the grinder of Gambart.

D. G. Rossetti

There is a creature called God
Whose creations are some of them odd.
I maintain and I shall,
The creation of Val
Reflects little credit on God.

Brigham Young was never a neutah,
A pansy or fairy or fruitah.
Where ten thousand virgins
Succumbed to his urgins
We now have the great state of Utah.

There was a young girl of Odessa
A rather unblushing transgressor.
When sent to the priest
The lewd little beast
Began to undress her confessor.

There was a young maid of Ostend
Who swore she'd hold out in the end.
But alas halfway over
From Calais to Dover
She done what she didn't intend.

There was an old maid of Pitlochry
Whose morals were truly a mockery,
For under her bed
Was a lover instead
Of the usual porcelain crockery.

A traveller to Timbuctoo
Said, "Pilot! It's time that we flew!"
He replied "That will do!
Your watch is askew:
It's a minute or two to 2:02."

A wonderful fish is the flea,
He bores and he bites on me.
I would love, indeed,
To watch him feed,
But he bites me where I cannot see.

An amoeba named Sam, and his brother
Were having a drink with each other.
In the midst of their quaffing,
They split themselves laughing,
And now each of them is a mother.

There was an old man of Blackheath,
Who sat on his set of false teeth.
Said he with a start,
"Oh lor, bless my heart!
I have bitten myself underneath."

There was a young lady from Coleshill
Who incautiously sat on a moleshill.
An inquisitive mole
Poked his nose up her hole.
The gal's OK but the mole's been a little off colour
since . . .

There once was a painter called Scott
Who seemed to have hair but had not.
He seemed to have sense
'Twas an equal pretence
On the part of the painter called Scott.

There's an Irishman Arthur O'Shaughnessy
On the chessboard of poets a pawn is he.
Though a bishop or king
Would be rather the thing
To the fancy of Arthur O'Shaughnessy.

A cannibal bold of Penzance
Ate an uncle and two of his aunts,
A cow and her calf,
An ox and a half,
And now he can't button his pants.

An eccentric old person of Slough
Who took all his meals with a cow,
Always said, "It's uncanny,
She's so like Aunt Fanny,"
But he would never indicate how.

There was an old lady of Brooking
Who had a great genius for cooking.
She could bake sixty pies,
All quite the same size,
And tell which was which without looking.

A visitor once to Loch Ness
Met the monster, who left him a mess.
They returned his entrails
By the regular mails
And the rest of the stuff by express.

There once was a man of Oporto
Who daily got shorter and shorter.
The reason, he said,
Was the hod on his head
Which was filled with the heaviest mortar.

Lewis Carroll

His sister Lucy O'Finner
Grew constantly thinner and thinner.
The reason was plain:
She slept out in the rain
And was never allowed any dinner.

There was a young fellow of Beaulieu
Who loved a fair maiden most treaulieu.
He said, "Do be mine,"
And she didn't decline,
So the wedding was solemnized deaulieu.

A charming young lady named Geoghegan,
Whose Christian names are less pagan,
Will be Mrs Knollys
Very soon at all Ksolly's
But the date is at present veogheg'un.

A young man of Gloucester named Foucester
Had a wife who ran off with a coster.
He traced her to Leicester
And tried to arrest her,
In spite of his efforts he lost her.

As he filled his order book pp.
He declared, "I demand higher ww."
So he struck for more pay
But, alas, they now say
He is sweeping out elephants cc.

There was a young lady called Psyche
Who was heard to ejaculate Pcryche!
For when riding her pbych,
She ran over a ptych
And fell on some rails that were pspyche.

There was a young lady of Whitby
Who had the bad luck to be bit by
Two brown little things
Without any wings
And now she's uncomfy to sit by.

~*~

A man hired by John Smith and Co.
Loudly declared that he'd tho.
Men that he saw
Dumping dirt near the door
The drivers, therefore, didn't do.

Mark Twain

~*~

A spelling reformer indicted
For fudge, was before the court cited.
The Judge said, "Enough!
Your candle we'll snough.
His sepulchre shall not be weighted."

There was a young genius of Queen's
Who was fond of exploding machines.
He once blew up a door,
But he'll do it no more,
For it chanced that the door was the Dean's.

There was an old fellow of Trinity,
A doctor well versed in divinity.
But he took to free thinking
And then to deep drinking
And so had to leave the vicinity.

There was a young critic of King's
Who had views on the limits of things.
With the size of his chapel
He would frequently grapple
And exclaim, "It's biggish for Kings!"

There was a young gourmand of John's
Who'd a notion of dining on swans.
To the Backs he took big nets
To capture the cygnets,
But was told they were kept for the dons.

A wonderful bird is the pelican,
His bill can hold more than his bellican,
He can take in his beak
Food enough for a week,
But I'm damned if I see how the helican.

There was a young man of Calcutta
Who had a most terrible stutter.
He said, "Pass the h h ham
And the j j j jam
and the b b b b b b butter."

There was a young curate of Kew
Who kept a tomcat in the pew.
He taught it to speak
Alphabetical Greek
But it never got further than miu.

The honourable Winifred Wemyss
Saw stylii and snakes in her dremyss,
And these she enjeud
Unytil she heard Freud
Say: "Nothing is quite as it semyss."

"I must leave here," said Lady De Vere,
"For these damp airs don't suit me, I fear."
Said her friend, "Goodness me!
If they don't agree
With your system, why eat pears, my dear?"

The tone-deaf old person of Tring,
When somebody asked him to sing,
Replied, "It is odd,
but I cannot tell *God
Save the Weasel* from *Pop goes the King*."

~◦❦◦~

There was a young lady of Ryde
Who ate some green apples and died.
The apples fermented
Inside the lamented,
And made cider inside her inside.

~◦❦◦~

There was a young fellow of Ceuta
Who rode into church on his scooter.
He knocked down the Dean
And said, "Sorry old bean!
I ought to have sounded my hooter!"

There was an old man of Boulogne
Who sang a most topical song;
It wasn't the words
Which frightened the birds
But the terrible double ontong.

There was a young man who said, "Ayer
Has answered the atheist's prayer,
For a hell one can't verify
Surely can't terrify
At least till you know you are there.

A dentist who lives in Duluth
Has wedded a widow named Ruth.
She is so sentimental
Concerning things dental,
She calls her dear second her "twoth."

There was a young lady of Cheadle
Who sat down in church on a needle.
Though deeply embedded
'Twas luckily threaded
So she had it removed by a beadle.

～･ﾞ･～

A baritone star of Havana
Slipped horribly on a banana.
He was sick for a year
Then resumed his career –
As a promising lyric soprano.

～･ﾞ･～

There once was a sculptor named Phidias
Who had a distaste for the hideous.
So he sculpt Aphrodite
Without any nightie
Which shocked the ultra-fastidious.

At Harvard, a naughty old Dean
Said, "The funniest jokes are obscene.
To bowdlerize wit
Takes the fun out of it –
Who wants a limerick clean?"

An authoress armed with a skewer
Once hunted a hostile reviewer.
"I'll teach him," she cried,
"When I've punctured his hide,
To call my last novel too pure."

"My girlfriend wants me to ski"
Said the flabby young cellist, "But Gee!
With Leopold Stokowski,
Mussorgsky, Tchaikovsky,
That's quite enough skiing for me."

There's an old Irish word meaning thief,
Four letters, quite pithy and brief.
I tell you no lie,
It's T-O-R-Y,
Now doesn't that beggar belief?

A fencing instructor called Fisk
In duel was terribly brisk.
So fast was his action
The Fitzgerald Contraction
Foreshortened his foil to a disc.

There was a faith healer of Deal
Who said, "Although pain isn't real,
If I sit on a pin
And it punctures my skin
I dislike what I fancy I feel."

There once was an eccentric old boffin
Who remarked in a fine fit of coughing,
"It isn't the cough
That carries you off,
But the coffin they carry you off in."

Of a sudden the great prima donna
Cried "Gawd, my voice is a gonner."
But a cat in the wings
Said, "I know how she sings,"
And finished the solo with honour.

Van Gogh, feeling devil-may-care
Labelled one of his efforts "The Chair."
No one knows if this bloke
Perpetrated a joke
Or the furniture needed repair.

An epicure dining at Crewe
Found a rather large mouse in his stew.
Said the waiter, "Don't shout,
Or wave it about,
Or the rest will be wanting one too."

On May Day the girls of Penzance
Being bored with the lack of romance,
Joined the workers' parade
With their banner displayed,
"What the pants of Penzance need is ants."

Two middle-aged ladies from Fordham
Went out for a walk but it bored 'em.
As they made their way back,
A sex maniac
Leapt out from some trees and ignored 'em.

There was a young girl of Tralee
Whose knowledge of French was "Oui Oui."
When they said, "Parlez-vous?"
She replied, "Same to you!"
She was famed for her bright repartee.

There was a young student called Jones
Who'd reduce any maiden to moans,
By his wonderful knowledge
Acquired in college
Of nineteen erogenous zones.

A menagerie came to Cape Race
Where they loved the gorilla's grimace.
He surprised them to learn
He owned the concern,
He was human in spite of his face.

A creature of charm is the gerbil.
Its diet is exclusively herbal,
It browses all day
On great bunches of hay
And farts with an elegant burble.

There once was a plesiosaurus
Who lived when the world was all porous.
But it fainted with shame
When it first heard its name
And departed long ages before us.

There was a young woman called Myrtle
Who once was seduced by a turtle.
The result of this mate
Was five crabs and a skate,
Thus proving the turtle was fertile.

There was an old lady of Wales
Who lived upon mussels and snails.
On growing a shell,
She exclaimed, "Just as well!
It will save me in bonnets and veils."

There was a young man named Steve
Whose manners were hard to believe.
He'd never say, "Please,"
Or beg pardon to sneeze,
And he'd shine up his shoes on your sleeve.

I know of a bellboy called Robbie
Who has a disgusting hobby.
Some think he's nuts
'Cause he saves all the butts
That he finds on the floor of the lobby.

There was an old man called Stan
Who put his foot in a pan
Of mustard and water,
Then got his young daughter
To cool off his face with a fan.

There was an old man from Bicester
Who was walking one day with his sister,
When a bull with one poke
Tossed her into an oak,
And the silly old bloke never missed her.

A bull in a china shop
Made the shopkeeper blow his top,
For this giant wild bison
Was breaking the Meissen
And no one could make it stop.

A hungry young man of Athlone
Had a great many reasons to moan.
His wife ate the ham
And the best leg of lamb,
So that all that was left was the bone.

A strapping young man named Howard
Was reputed to be muscle-powered.
But when a small mouse
Crept into the house
He jumped on the table, the coward.

There was a young man of Devizes
Whose appearance was full of surprises.
His nose was askew
Only one eye was blue
And his eyes quite different sizes.

There was a young boy of Quebec
Who was buried in snow to his neck.
When asked, "Are you frizz?"
He replied , "Yes I is,
But we don't call this cold in Quebec."

R. Kipling

There was a young girl of Shanghai
Who was so exceedingly shy,
That undressing at night
She turned out the light
For fear of the all-seeing eye.

Bertrand Russell

There was an old man of Lyme
Who married three wives at a time.
When asked "Why a third?"
He replied, "One's absurd!
And bigamy, Sir, is a crime."

In the garden of Eden lay Adam,
Complacently stroking his Madam,
And loud was his mirth
For he knew that on Earth
There were only two balls and he had 'em.

A sculptor remarked, "I'm afraid
I've fallen in love with my trade.
I'm much too elated
With what I've created,
And, chiefly, the women I've made."

There is a young lady named Aird
Whose bottom is always kept bared.
When asked why, she pouts,
And says the Boy Scouts
All beg her please to Be Prepared.

An old maid in the land of Aloa
Got wrapped in the coils of a boa.
And as the snake squeezed,
The old maid, not displeased,
Cried, "Darling! I love it! Samoa!"

An amorous maiden Antique
Locked a man in her house for a week.
He entered the door
With a shout and a roar
But his exit was marked by a squeak.

There was a young man from Australia
Who painted his ass like a dahlia.
The colour was fine,
Likewise the design,
The aroma, ah, that was a failia.

A very wise lady called Anne
Would have nothing to do with a man.
Until a pools winner
Took her out to dinner
And flew her off to Japan.

An ancient knight called Lancelot
Was known by all to glance alot
At Queen Guinevere
Even call her "My dear,"
And take her out to dance alot.

A thoughtful young man named Clem
Picked a rose from a stem.
He gave it to Alice,
Who said without malice,
"I'd rather have cash or a gem."

There was a man called Neville
Who claimed to be on the level.
But when he kissed Sue,
He gave me one too,
That Neville is rather a devil.

A nautical man from Dundee
Devotedly wooed Miss Elly,
Till one evening in summertime,
She said, "Bill it's maritime,"
And he immediately left for the sea.

There now lives a man in Perth
Who had a very strange birth.
His ears kept on growing,
His eyes are both glowing,
Could it be he's not from this earth?

I know a man called Calhoun
Whose belly is like a balloon.
He's dark, not fair,
And he's covered in hair,
And looks just like a baboon.

There was a kid named Sid
Who lived in Spanish Madrid.
The things that he did,
This kid from Madrid,
To know you must pay me a quid.

There was a young man of Woods Hole
Who had an affair with a mole.
He was a bit of a nancy
But he did like to fancy
Himself in the dominant role.

Said an ape as he swung by his tail,
To his offspring both male and female,
"From your offspring, my dears,
In a couple of years,
May evolve a professor at Yale."

A herder who hailed from Terre Haute
Fell in love with a young nanny goat.
The daughter he sired
Was greatly admired
For her beautiful angora coat.

There were three little owls in a wood
Who sang hymns whenever they could.
What the words were about
One could never make out
But one felt it was doing them good.

There was a young lady in white
Who looked out in the depth of the night.
But the birds of the air
Filled her with despair,
And depressed that young lady in white.

Concerning the bees and the flowers
In the fields and the gardens and bowers,
You will tell at a glance
That their ways of romance
Haven't any resemblance to ours.

There once were two cats of Kilkenny
Each thought there was one cat too many.
So they quarrelled and fit,
They scratched and they bit,
Till barring their nails
And the tips of their tails,
Instead of two cats there weren't any.

There was an old man with a beard
Who said, "It's just as I feared!
Two owls and a hen,
Four larks and a wren,
Have all made their nests in my beard!"

～❦～

A certain young chap named Bill Beebee
Was in love with a lady named Phoebe.
"But," he said "I must see
What the clerical fee
Be before Phoebe be Phoebe B. Beebee."

～❦～

A flea and a fly in the flue
Were imprisoned so what could they do?
Said the fly, "Let us flee,"
Said the flea, "Let us fly!"
So they flew through a flaw in the flue.

There's a wonderful family called Stein,
There's Gert and there's Ep and there's Ein.
Gert's poems are bunk,
Ep's statues are junk,
And no one can understand Ein.

A short-sighted man from Havana
Confused clothing with flora and fauna.
He was heard to say "Ouch!"
When a black posing pouch
Turned out to be three small piranha.

I once thought a lot of a friend
Who turned out to be in the end
The southernmost part
(As I feared from the start)
Of a horse with a northerly trend.

A newspaper writer called Fling
Could make copy from most anything.
But the copy he wrote
Of a ten-dollar note
Was so good he is now in Sing Sing.

There was a young lady of Crewe
Who wanted to catch the 2:02.
Said a porter, "Don't worry
Or hurry or scurry,
It's a minute or two to 2:02."

The thoughts of the rabbit on sex,
Are seldom, if ever, complex.
For a rabbit in need
Is a rabbit in deed
And does just as a person expects.

"I shall star," vowed a girl from Biloxi
"At Twentieth Century Foxi,"
And her movie career
Really prospered last year:
She's in charge of the mops at the Roxy.

There was a young man by the Nile
Who decided he'd swim for a while.
But why did he pause?
He saw the great jaws
Of a perfectly huge crocodile.

You musn't try to grab
A very bad-tempered crab.
For if you do,
I'm telling you,
Its pincers will give you a jab.

Said a very outspoken lass
Who liked to abuse and harass,
"My dear, your ears
Have been growing for years,
And you're getting to look like an ass."

A sensitive lady of Chelsea
Spent a weekend at Selsea.
When asked if alone
She said, "Mind your own,
I'm just not going to tell, see!"

A batsman who was on the large side
Was heckled by an opponent who cried,
"When he's at the wicket,
It's not really cricket
Is that what you mean by a wide?"

In skool exams I'm excelling
So I rote my mother foretelling
All the results mite
Be kwite all rite,
Well, except perhaps for my speling.

I told a joke to my pa.
He listened and said, "Ha ha,
Ha ha, ha ha,
Ha ha, ha ha
Ha ha . . . vn't you got anything better to do than waste
your time telling me jokes that aren't even very
funny?"

There was an old lady of Lincoln
Who made a considerable stink on
The subject of furs,
For that young niece of hers
Had run off with nothing but mink on.

Chapter 3

~•~

MY MOTHER CAME FROM HUNSTANTON

A publisher went off to France
In search of a tale of romance.
A Parisian lady
Told a story so shady
That the publisher made an advance.

Finding clean limericks is a bit like finding perfect blackberries: September hedges might seem plump with berries, but finding a blackberry that is the right size, maggot-free, ripe and within reach is not easy. In this chapter we've struck lucky and there are lots of limericks for the whole family to enjoy.

A drunken old tar from St Clements
To ward off the scurvy sucked lemons.
"With my health unimpaired
I'll have time," he declared
"To die of delirium tremens."

There was a young man so benighted
He never knew when he was slighted.
He went to a party,
And ate just as hearty
As if he'd been really invited.

There was a co-ed of Cayenne
Who ate onions, blue cheese and sen-sen.
Till a bad fright one day
Took her breath quite away,
And we hope she won't find it again.

There was a young lady of Herm
Who tied bows on the tail of a worm.
She said, "You look festive,
But don't become restive,
You'll wriggle them off if you squirm."

There was a young lady named Bright
Who travelled far faster than light.
She set out one day
In a relative way
And returned on the previous night.

"The order of nature," quoth he
"Is wondrously brought home to me
When I think that my clock
With each tick and each tock
Goes $2\pi\sqrt{\frac{1}{g}}$"

(two pi times the root of 1 over g)

There was an old woman of Lynn
Whose nose very near reached her chin.
You may easy suppose
She had plenty of beaux
This charming old woman of Lynn.

There was an old woman of Gloucester
Whose parrot two guineas it cost her.
But his tongue never ceasing
Was vastly displeasing
To that talkative woman of Gloucester.

There was a sick man of Tobago
Lived long on rice gruel and sago.
But at last, to his bliss,
The physician said this,
"To a roast leg of mutton you may go."

I shall with cultured taste
Distinguish gems from paste,
And "High diddle diddle"
Will rank as an idyll
If I pronounce it chaste!

W. S. Gilbert

An unfortunate dumb mute from Kew
Was trying out sounds that he knew.
He did them so fast
That his fingers at last
Got so tangled he fractured a few.

Some amateur players so brave,
A performance of Hamlet once gave.
Said a wag, "Now let's see
If it's Bacon or he –
I mean Shakespeare – who's turned in his grave."

Miss Vera de Peyster Depew
Disdained anything that was new.
She said, "I do not
Know exactly what's what,
But I know without question Who's Who."

Two beauties who dwelt by the Bosphorus
Had eyes that were brighter than phosphorus.
The Sultan cried, "Troth!
I'd marry you both!"
But they laughed, "I'm afraid you'll have to toss for us."

An important young man from Quebec
Had to welcome the Duchess of Treck.
So he bought for a dollar
A very high collar
To save himself washing his neck.

There was an old widower Doyle
Who wrapped his wife in tin foil.
He thought it would please her
To stay in the freezer
And anyway, outside she'd spoil.

There was an old fellow from Croydon
Whose cook was a cute little hoyden.
She would sit on his knees
While shelling the peas
Or pleasanter duties employed on.

Rebecca, a silly young wench,
Went on to the Thames to catch tench.
When the boat was upset,
She exclaimed, I regret,
A five-letter word, and in French.

There was an old maid of Genoa,
And I blush when I think what I owe her.
She's gone to her rest
And it's all for the best,
Otherwise I could borrow Samoa.

An oyster from Kalamazoo
Confessed he was feeling quite blue.
For he said, "As a rule,
When the weather turns cool,
I invariably get in a stew."

To his wife said a grumbler named Dutton,
"I'm a gourmet, I am, not a glutton.
For ham, jam or lamb
I don't give a damn,
So come on, let's return to our mutton."

Said a foolish householder of Wales,
"An odour of coal gas prevails."
She then struck a light
And later that night
Was collected in seventeen pails.

There was a young man at the war office
Whose brain was as good as a store office.
Every warning severe
Simply went in one ear
And out of the opposite orifice.

There was a good canon of Durham
Who fished with a hook and a worrum.
Said the Dean to the Bishop,
"I've brought a big fish up,
But I fear we will have to inter 'im."

There was an old lady of Rye,
Who was baked by mistake in a pie.
To the householder's disgust
She emerged in the crust
And exclaimed with a yawn, "Where am I?"

There's a lady in Kalamazoo
Who first bites her oyster in two.
She has a misgiving,
Should any be living,
They'd raise such a hullabaloo.

They say that I was, in my youth,
Uncouth and ungainly, forsooth.
I can only reply,
" 'Tis a lie, 'tis a lie!
I was couth, I was perfectly couth."

There was a brave damsel of Brighton
Whom nothing could possibly frighten.
She plunged in the sea
And, with infinite glee,
Sailed away on the back of a Triton.

There was a young lady of Venice
Who used hard-boiled eggs to play tennis.
People said, "That is wrong."
She replied "Get along!
You don't know how prolific my hen is."

There was a young girl of West Ham
Who hastily jumped on a tram.
When she had embarked
The conductor remarked,
"Your fare, miss." She answered "I am."

There was an old lady of Kent,
Whose nose was remarkably bent.
One day, they suppose,
She followed her nose,
And no one knew which way she went.

The village was giddy with rumours
Of a goat who was suffering from tumours.
Cans and library paste
Were quite to her taste
But she choked on Elizabeth's bloomers.

There was an old woman of Filey
Who valued old candle ends highly.
When no one was looking
She'd use them for cooking –
"It's wicked to waste," she said dryly.

Well, if it's a sin to like Guinness,
Then that, I admit's what my sin is.
I like it with fizz
Or just as it is
And it's much better for me than gin is.

A Turk by the name of Haroun
Ate whisky by means of a spoon.
When someone asked, "Why?"
He gave this reply,
"To drink is forbidden, you loon."

A major, with wonderful force,
Called out in Hyde Park for a horse.
All the flowers looked round
But not one could be found,
So he just rhododendron of course.

A glutton from Bingen-am-Rhein
Was asked at what hour he would dine.
He replied, "At eleven,
At three, five and seven,
And eight, and a quarter to nine.

A dancing girl came to St Gall,
With a mouth so exceedingly small.
That she said, "It could be
Much more easy for me
To do without eating at all."

There was a young lady of Lynn
Who was so uncommonly thin
That when she essayed
To drink lemonade
She slipped through the straw and fell in.

A horrible brat from Belgravia
Drove his parents to thoughts of Our Saviour.
"By Jesus," they swore,
"We can't stand much more
Of this sonofabitch's behaviour."

The mouth of a glutton named Moto
Was the size that no organ should grow to.
It could take with ease
Six carrots, ten peas,
And a whole baked potato in toto.

There was an old skinflint called Green
Who grew so abnormally lean
And flat and compressed
That his back squeezed his chest,
And sideways he couldn't be seen.

A housewife called out with a frown,
When surprised by some callers in town:
"In a minute or less
I'll slip on a dress,"
But she slipped on the stairs and then died.

There was a young lady of Kent
Who always said just what she meant.
People said, "She's a dear –
So unique, so sincere,"
But they shunned her by common consent.

A publisher went off to France
In search of a tale of romance.
A Parisian lady
Told a story so shady
That the publisher made an advance.

A singer in Radio City
(Whose form is impressively pretty)
Is often addressed
By the name of Beau Chest
Which is thought to be tasteful and witty.

~❧~

There was a young fellow named Willie
Who acted remarkably silly.
At an all-nations ball
Dressed in nothing at all
He claimed his costume was Chile.

~❧~

Said the crow to the pelican, "Grant
Me the loan of your bill, for my aunt
Has asked me to tea."
Said the other, "Not me,
Ask my brother – for this pelican't."

A painter who lived in Great Britain
Interrupted two girls at their knitting.
Said he with a sigh,
"That park bench, er, I
Just painted it right where you're sitting."

There once was a sailor named Pink
Whose mates rushed him off to the clink.
Said he, "I've a skunk
As a pet in my bunk
But that's no reason for raising a stink."

There was a young man of Westphalia
Who yearly got tail-ier and tail-ier,
When he took on the shape
Of a Barbary ape
With the consequent paraphernalia.

There once was a baby of yore
Whose parents found it a bore
And, being afraid
It might be mislaid,
They stored it away in a drawer.

Despite her impressive physique
Fatima was really quite meek.
If a mouse showed its head
She would jump into bed
With a terrible bloodcurdling shriek.

A lady removing her scanties
Heard them crackle electrical chanties.
Said her husband, "My dear,
I very much fear
You suffer from amps in your panties."

A contemptuous matron from Shoreham
Behaved with extreme indecorum.
    She snapped a sarcastic
    And secret elastic
Throughout the community forum.

A Korean whose home was in Seoul
Had notions uncommonly droll.
    He'd get himself stewed
    And pose in the nude
On top of the telegraph pole.

There once was a girl from Revere
So enormously large that, oh dear!
    Once far out in the ocean
    Byrd raised a commotion
By planting our flag on her rear.

A singular fellow of Weston
Has near fifty feet of intestine,
Though a signal success
In the medical press
It isn't much good for digestin'.

There was a young woman of Thrace
Whose nose spread all over her face.
She had very few kisses,
The reason for this is
There wasn't a suitable place.

A Tory, once out in his motor,
Ran over a Labourite voter.
"Thank goodness," he cried
"He was on the wrong side.
So I don't blame myself one iota."

A sleeper from the Amazon
Put nighties of his grandma's on
The reason: that
He was too fat
To get his own pyjamazon.

A two-toothed old man of Arbroath
Gave vent to a terrible oath.
When one tooth chanced to ache
By an awful mistake,
The dentists extracted them both.

There was a young man from Tacoma
Whose breath had a whisky aroma.
So to alter the smell
He swallowed Chanel
And went off in a heavenly coma.

A hapless church tenor was Horace,
Whose skin was so terribly porous,
Sometimes in the choir
He'd start to perspire
And nearly drown out the whole chorus.

A God-fearing maiden from Goshen
Took a September-morn swim in the ocean.
When a whirlpool appeared
She rose up and cheered
And developed a rotary motion.

Have you heard about Madame Upescu
Who came to Romania's rescue?
It's a wonderful thing
To be under a king,
Is democracy better I ask you?

A French poodle espied in the hall
A pool that a damp gamp let fall.
And said, "Ah oui oui!
This time it's not me,
But I'm bound to be blamed for it all."

An adventurous fun-loving polyp
Propositioned a cute little scallop
Down under the sea.
"Nothing doing," said she;
"By Triton – you think I'm a trollop."

There was a young lady of Ealing
Who walked up and down on the ceiling.
She shouted, "Oh heck!
I've broken my neck,
And it is a peculiar feeling."

There once were some learned MDs
Who captured some germs of disease
And infected a train,
Which, without causing pain,
Allowed one to catch it with ease.

There was a young man of Madras
Possessed of a beautiful ass.
It was not round and pink
As you possibly think
But was grey, had long ears, and ate grass.

There was a young cashier of Calais
Whose accounts, when reviewed, wouldn't tally,
So his chief smelt a rat
For he'd furnished a flat,
And was seen every night at the balais.

There was a young lady of Rye,
With a shape like a capital I.
When they told her she had,
She learned how to pad
Which shows just how figures can lie.

There was an old lady of Seaton
Who asked for a chair, once she'd eaten.
When told by her son,
"You're sitting on one,"
Said she, "It's for putting my feet on."

A grandmother who couldn't be sterner
Grabbed her grandaughter and threatened to burn her.
The girl seized the cat
And said, "Granny, burn that,"
For at cruelty that girl was a learner.

There was a young man from Calcutta
Who constantly ate peanut butter.
His mother would say
To his father each day,
"I'm sure that our son is a nutter."

I knew a girl named Florence
Who held in great abhorrence
The work she did
For uncle Sid
As well as uncle Lawrence.

There was a young lady of Strood
Who was mighty fussy with food.
The meat she would eat
(An occasional treat)
Had to be carefully stewed.

A millionaire's son went on trips
In jets and luxury ships.
But all he would eat
In cold or in heat
Were platefuls of burgers and chips.

There once was a young man who'd feast
On nothing but lumps of fresh yeast.
It was hard in the morn
To rise up at dawn
But the yeast got him started at least.

There was a young curate of Minster
Who admonished a giddy young spinster.
For she used, on the ice,
Words not at all nice
When he at a turn, slid against her.

There was a young parson called Perkins,
Exceedingly fond of small gherkins.
One summer at tea
He ate forty-three,
Which pickled his internal workings.

There was an old codger of Broome
Who kept a baboon in his room.
"It reminds me," he said
"Of a friend who is dead."
But he never would tell us of whom.

God's plan made a hopeful beginning
But man spoiled his chances by sinning.
We trust that the story
Will end in God's glory,
But at present the other side's winning.

A nudist resort in Benares
Took a midget in all unawares.
But he made members weep
For he just couldn't keep
His nose out of private affairs.

A lisping young lady named Beth
Was saved from a fate worse than death
Seven times in a row,
Which unsettled her so
That she quit saying "No" and said "Yeth."

There was a young parson named Bings
Who talked about God and things.
But his secret desire
Was a boy in the choir
With a bottom like jelly on springs.

A young trapeze artist named Bract
Is faced by a very sad fact.
Imagine his pain,
When again and again,
He catches his wife in the act.

An indolent vicar of Bray
His roses allowed to decay.
His wife, more alert,
Brought a powerful squirt
And said to her spouse, "Let us spray."

There was a young lady of Ash
Who always ate bangers and mash.
She found that sweet jelly
Would fatten her belly
And make her break out in a rash.

Chapter 4

~❧~

NAUGHTY LIMERICKS

Cheeky is perhaps the best word to describe the limericks in this and the following chapters. One of the wonderful aspects of limericks is that the reader can be led a merry dance. Rhymes can suggest that something might be about to happen that you don't really want to hear, but the best ones veer suddenly onto quite a different track, leaving you slightly breathless and a little relieved.

When twins came, their father, Dan Dunn,
Gave Edward as name to each son.
When folks cried, "Absurd!"
He replied, "Ain't you heard
That two Eds are better than one?"

There was a young lady of Harwich
Whose conduct was odd at her marriage.
She proceeded on skates
To the parish church gates
While her friends followed on in a carriage.

A famous theatrical actress
Played best in the role of malefactress.
Yet her home life was pure
Except, to be sure
A scandal or two just for practice.

There was a young woman named Frances
Who decided to better his chances
By cleverly adding
Appropriate padding
To enlarge all her protuberances.

There was a young lady of Clyde
Whose shoelaces once came untied.
She feared that to bend
Would display her rear end
So she cried and she cried and she cried.

There was a fat man of Lahore,
The same shape behind as before.
They did not know where
To offer a chair,
So he had to sit down on the floor.

An impish young fellow named James
Had a passion for idiot games.
He lighted the hair
Of his lady's affair
And laughed as she peed out the flames.

There was an old fellow of Tyre
Who constantly sat on the fire.
When asked, "Are you hot?"
He said, "Certainly not,
I'm James Winterbottom Esquire."

A certain young laddie named Robbie
Rode his steed back and forth in the lobby.
When they told him, "Indoors
Is no place for a horse."
He replied, "Well you see it's my hobby."

Said the Duke to the Duchess of Avery,
"Forgive me for breaking your reverie.
You've been sitting on Punch
Since long before lunch –
Might I have it before it's unsavoury?"

Said a fair-headed maiden of Klondike,
"Of you I'm exceedingly fond, Ike.
To prove I adore you,
I'll die, darling, for you,
And be a brunette, not a blonde, like."

A lady on climbing Mount Shasta
Complained as the mountain grew vaster
That it wasn't the climb
Nor the dirt nor the grime
But the ice on her ass that harassed her.

A certain young lady called Hannah
Was caught in a flood in Montana.
As she floated away
Her beau, so they say,
Accompanied her on the piannah.

There was a young farmer named Max
Who avoided the gasoline tax.
It was simple you see,
For his Vespa burned pee
From his grandfather's herd of tame yaks.

A disgusting young man named McGill
Made his neighbours increasingly ill
When they learned of his habits
Involving white rabbits
And a bird with a flexible bill.

There was an old man who said, "Please,
Give me some of your Cotherstone cheese.
I have smelt it for miles
Coming over the stiles
To your charming farmhouse on the Tees."

There once was a damsel named Jinx
Who, when asked what she thought of the Sphinx,
Replied with a smile,
"That old fraud by the Nile?
I personally think that he stinks."

An eccentric old spinster named Lowell
Announced to her friends "Bless my sowell,
I've gained so much weight,
I am sorry to state,
I fear I am going to be fowell."

As they fished his old plane from the sea,
The inventor just chortled with glee.
"I shall build" and he laughed,
"A submarine craft,
And perhaps it will fly, we shall see."

There was a young charmer named Sheba,
Whose pet was a darling amoeba.
This queer blob of jelly
Would lie on her belly
And blissfully murmur "Ich liebe."

Our vicar is good mister Inge.
One evening he offered to sing.
So we asked him to stoop,
Put his head in a loop
And pulled at each end of the string.

A classical scholar from Flint
Devised a curious squint.
With her left-handed eye
She could scan the whole sky
While the other was reading small print.

There once was a boy from Baghdad,
An inquisitive sort of a lad.
He said, "Let us see
If a sting has a bee,"
And he very soon found that it had.

The conquering Lion of Judah
Made a prayer to the statue of Buddha.
"Oh, Idol," he prayed,
"May Il Duçe be spayed,
And all his descendants be neuter."

There was a young lady of Wilts
Who walked to the Highlands on stilts.
When they said, "Oh how shocking,
To show so much stocking!"
She answered "Well how about kilts?"

~⁂~

A vessel has sailed from Chicago,
With barrels of pork for a cargo.
For Boston she's bound,
Preceded I've found,
By another with beans from near Fargo.

~⁂~

A bibulous chap from Duquesne
Drank a whole jeroboam of champagne.
Said he with a laugh
As he quaffed the last quaff,
"I tried to get drunk, but in vain."

In the days of mild Gerry Ford
Decorum and calm were restored.
He did nothing hateful,
For which we were grateful
And terribly, terribly bored.

"What have I done?" said Christine.
"I've ruined the party machine.
To lie in the nude
Is not very rude,
But to lie in the house is obscene."

There was an old man of Tarentum
Who gnashed his false teeth till he bent 'em.
When they asked him the cost
Of what he had lost
He replied, "I can't say, I just rent 'em."

There's a clever old miser who tries
Every method to economize.
He said with a wink,
"I save gallons of ink
By simply not dotting my i's."

There was a young dandy of Bute
Who sported a very loud suit.
When told "It's too loud,"
He archly said, "How'd
I look in a suit that was mute?"

There was a young lady of Cheltenham
Put on tights just to see how she felt in 'em.
But she said with a shout,
"If you don't pull me out,
I'm sure I'll jolly soon melt in 'em."

There was an old lady who said,
When she found a thief under her bed,
"So near the floor,
And so close to the door!
I'm afraid you'll catch cold in your head."

A statesman who lives near the Isis
Remarked to his cook in a crisis,
"This meat is so tough
It is more than enough
To give a gas oven gastritis."

A minister up in Vermont
Keeps goldfish alive in his font.
When he dips the babes in
It tickles the skin,
Which is all that the innocent want.

There were once three fellows from Gary,
Named Larry, Harry, and Barry,
Now Harry was bare
As an egg or a pear,
But Barry and Larry were hairy.

There was a young lady of Crete
Who was so exceedingly neat.
When she got out of bed
She stood on her head
To make sure of not soiling her feet.

There was a young man who was bitten
By twenty-two cats and a kitten.
Cried he, "It is clear
My end is quite near!
No matter, I'll die like a Briton."

There was an old woman of Clewer
Who was riding a bike and it threw her.
A butcher came by
And said, "Missus, don't cry,"
And fixed her back on with a skewer.

An unfortunate lady named Piles
Had the ugliest bottom for miles.
But her surgeon took pity
And made it quite pretty,
All dimples, poutings and smiles.

A slumbering infant named Daniel
Dreamt his leg had been bit by a spaniel.
He awoke from his dream
With a bloodcurdling scream.
Said the nursery maid, "My! That boy can yell."

There was a dear lady of Eden
Who on apples was quite fond of feeding.
She gave one to Adam
Who said, "Thank you, Madam,"
And then both skedaddled from Eden.

There was a girl from New York
Whose body was lighter than cork.
She had to be fed
For six weeks upon lead
Before she went out for a walk.

There was an old man who said, "Do
Tell me how I'm to add two and two.
I'm not very sure
That it doesn't make four,
But I fear it's almost too few."

There was a young friar called Borrow
Who eloped with two nuns, to his sorrow.
They lived on an isthmus
And one he named Christmas,
The other he christened Tomorrow.

There once lived a certain Miss Gale
Who turned most exceedingly pale.
For a mouse climbed her leg
(Don't repeat this I beg)
And a splinter got caught in its tail.

There was a young person named Tate
Took a girl out to eat at 8:08.
But I will not relate
What Tate and his date
Ate, tête-à-tête at 8:08.

There was an old man of Peru
Who dreamt he was eating his shoe.
He woke in the night
In a terrible fright
And found it was perfectly true.

～·👂·～

A clergyman told from his text
How Samson was scissored and vexed.
Then a barber arose
From his sweet Sunday doze
Got rattled and shouted, "Who's next?"

～·👂·～

There was a young fellow named Sydney,
Who drank till he ruined his kidney.
It shrivelled and shrank
As he sat there and drank,
But he had a good time at it, didn't he?

There was a young golfer at Troon
Who always played golf with a spoon.
"It's handy you see,
For the brandy you see,
Should anyone happen to swoon."

The great violinist was bowing,
The quarrelsome oarsmen were rowing.
But how is the sage
To judge from the page
Was it pigs or seeds that were sowing?

A foreigner said, "I have heard
Your language is really absurd.
The spelling is weird,
Much worse than I feared,
For word rhymes with bird, nerd or curd."

The Vikings had sagas of yore
Of monsters, and hunting the boar.
The poems he said
Were all in his head.
No wonder his spelling was pour.

There was a young farmer from Slough
Who said, "I've a terrible cough.
Do you think I should get
Both the doc and the vet,
Or would one be enough for now?"

There was a young man named Colquhoun
Who kept as a pet a baboon
His mother said, "Cholmondeley,
I don't think it's quite comely
To feed your baboon with a spoon."

There was an old person of Fratton
Who would go to church with his hat on
"When I wake up," he said
"With my hat on my head,
I shall know that it hasn't been sat on."

A mosquito was heard to complain
That a chemist had poisoned his brain.
The cause of his sorrow
Was paradichloro-
Diphenyltrichloroethane.

A decrepit old gasman named Peter,
While hunting around his gas heater,
Touched a leak with his light.
He rose out of sight
And, as everyone who knows anything about poetry
can tell you, he ruined the metre.

We thought him an absolute lamb,
But when he sat down on the jam
On taking his seat
At the Sunday school treat
We all heard the vicar say, "Stand up please,
While I say grace."

There was a young lady called Kent
Who gave up her husband for Lent.
The night before Easter
When Jesus released her,
It didn't make a damned bit of difference because in
the meantime he'd been running around with a whole
lot of other women.

A right-handed writer named Wright
In writing "write" always wrote "rite"
When he meant to write "write."
If he'd written "write" right,
Wright would not have wrought rot writing "rite."

Said a boy to his teacher one day,
"Wright has not written 'rite' right, I say."
And the teacher replied,
As the error she eyed,
"Right! Wright: write 'write' right, right away."

An unskilful rider from Rhyl
Motorcycled full speed down a hill.
Till a spill at a bend
Killed our wilful young friend,
And he now in the churchyard lies still.

A wandering tribe called the Siouxs
Wear moccasins, having no shiouxs.
They are made of buckskin
With the fleshy side in,
Embroidered with beads of bright hiouxs.

There was a young curate of Salisbury
Whose habits were halisbury-scalisbury.
He'd go hiking in Hampshire
Without any pampshire
Till the bishop insisted he walisbury.

There was a young lady from Slough
Who drank her milk straight from the cow.
To her udder delight
She could drink through the night,
Amazing, but don't ask me how.

There was a young cannibal, Joe
Who used to eat plates of cod's roe.
His mother said, "Sonny,
It's not very funny,
You ought to eat people you know."

There was a young man of Yalding
Who liked to drink tea when it's scalding.
The result of this heat
Was pigeon-toed feet
And a head that was rapidly balding.

There was an old lady of Norwich
Whose diet was high in roughage.
She was terribly keen
On the common baked bean,
And she got the wind up with porridge.

Waiter, this soup has a smell,
Reminiscent of brimstone from hell.
The taste is as foul
As a decomposed owl
And it looks like green slime as well.

There was an old lady of Harrow
Who rode into church on a barrow.
When she stuck in the aisle
Said she, with a smile,
"They build these 'ere churches too narrow."

A remarkable feature has Myrtle,
A retractable tail like a turtle.
But though she has never
Been called cute or clever,
She annually proves to be fertile.

There was an old person of Prague
Who was suddenly seized with the ague.
But they gave him some butter
Which caused him to stutter
And cured the old person's plague.

The bottle of perfume that Willie sent
Was highly displeasing to Millicent.
Her thanks were so cold
They quarrelled I'm told
Through the silly scent Willy sent Millicent.

A schoolboy at Sault Ste Marie
Said, "Spelling is all Greek to me,
Till they learn to spell 'Soo'
Without any 'u'
Or an 'a' or an 'l' or a 't'."

An amorous girl called Kate
Was told she'd have to wait
For the fruit of the palm
But she learned with alarm
That her wait made her late for her date.

There once was a choleric Colonel
Whose oaths were obscene and infolonel.
As the chaplain, aghast,
Gave up protest at last,
But wrote it all down in his jolonel.

A fellow who lived in New Guinea
Was known as a silly young nuinea.
He utterly lacked
Good judgment and tacked
For he told a plump girl she was skuinea.

A bright little maid of St Thomas
Discovered a suit of pyjamas.
Said the maiden, "Well, well,
Whose they are I can't tell
But I'm sure those garments aren't mama's."

There were two young ladies of Birmingham
And I know a sad story concerningham.
They stuck needles and pins
In the right reverend shins
Of the bishop engaged in confirminham.

There was a young girl in the choir
Whose voice rose hoir and hoir,
Till it reached such a height
It was clear out of sight
And they found it next day in the spoir.

There was a composer named Liszt
Whose music no one could resist.
When he swept the keyboard
Nobody could be bored
And now that he's gone he is missed.

My name is John Wellington Wells,
I'm a dealer in magic and spells,
In blessings and curses,
And ever-filled purses,
In prophesies, witches and knells.

W. S. Gilbert

There was a professor named Chesterton,
Who went for a walk with his best shirt on.
Being hungry he ate it,
But lived to regret it,
And ruined for life his digestion.

The Reverend Henry Ward Beecher
Called a hen a most elegant creature.
The hen, pleased with that
Laid an egg in his hat,
And thus did the hen reward Beecher.

'Tis strange how the newspapers honour
A creature that's called prima donna.
They say not a thing
Of how she can sing
But reams of the clothes she has on her.

Now what in the world shall we dioux
With the bloody and murderous Sioux
Who, some time ago
Took an arrow and a bow
And raised such a hellabalioux?

Eugene Field

A silly young girl named Fiona
Was oh such a moaner and groaner.
One day in despair,
She pulled out her hair
And now no man ever phones her.

There was a young lady of Whitby
Who had the luck to be hit by
Two brown little things
Without any wings
And now she's uncomfy to sit by.

In Paris some visitors go
To see what no person should know.
And then there are tourists,
The purest of purists
Who say it is quite comme il faut.

A skeleton once in Khartoum
Invited a ghost to his room.
They spent the whole night
In the eeriest fight
As to who should be frightened of whom.

A fancy meat packer named Young
One day, when his nerves were unstrung,
    Pushed his wife's ma unseen
    In the chopping machine
Then canned her and labelled her "Tongue."

Said a widow whose singular vice
Was to keep her late husband on ice,
    "It's been hard since I lost him –
    I'll never defrost him!
Cold comfort, but cheap at the price."

There was a young fellow called Hall
Who fell in the spring in the fall.
    "'Twould have been a sad thing,
    Had he died in the spring
But he didn't, he died in the fall."

There was an old man in a hearse
Who murmured, "This might have been worse.
Of course the expense
Is simply immense,
But it doesn't come out of my purse."

There was a young man from Kilbride
Who fell down a sewer and died.
Now he had a brother
Who fell down another,
And now they're interred side by side.

A golfer now out on the links
Stops play at each tea for drinks.
Take it from me,
The drink isn't tea,
But a cocktail they call Hi Jinx.

A cricketer of considerable fame
Dishonestly earned his acclaim.
By cheating at cricket
And gluing his wicket
He'd always win all of his games.

There once was a great big black cat
Who swallowed a whole cricket bat.
He swallowed the ball,
The stumps, bail and all,
So the cricket team clobbered him flat.

There was a young fellow named Brett
Loved a girl in his shiny Corvette.
We know it's absurd
But the last that we heard
They hadn't untangled them yet.

A delighted incredulous bride
Remarked to the groom at her side,
"I never could quite
Believe till tonight
Our anatomies would coincide."

An Argentine gaucho named Bruno
Once said, "There is one thing I do know:
A woman is fine,
A sheep is divine,
But a llama is numero uno."

There was a young lady of Ryde
Whose locks were considerably dyed.
The hue of her hair
Made everyone stare
"She's piebald, she'll die bald!" they cried.

A cynic of much savoir faire
Pursued by a horrible bear,
Said, "I'll argue a while
In the feminine style.
No creature could follow me there."

You will find by the banks of the Nile
The haunts of the great crocodile.
He will welcome you in
With an innocent grin
Which gives way to a satisfied smile.

At the zoo I remarked to an emu
"I cannot pretend I esteem you.
You're a greedy old bird
And your walk is absurd
Not even your feathers redeem you."

The kings of Peru were the Incas,
Who were known far and wide as great drinkers.
They worshiped the sun,
And had lots of fun,
But the peons all thought them great stinkers.

Fishermen and footballers get
Plenty of sport, you can bet.
Whether it's a goal,
Or a great Dover sole,
They'll shout, "It's now in the net."

There was a swimmer from Sale
Who was hit on the nose by a whale.
It happened at Rhyl
Said she, "What a thrill,
I'm still living to tell the tale."

There was a young bather called Mark
Who saw the fin of a shark.
He said, "The deep sea
Is no place for me,
I'll swim in the lake in the park."

A bakery student named Jake
Decided that he could make
A quick buck or two
If he married sweet Sue
Then charged her dad for the cake.

The man who invented the sprocket,
Went on to develop the socket.
Then one afternoon
He went to the moon,
That's right, he'd invented the rocket.

Chapter 5

VERY NAUGHTY LIMERICKS

Calling into question a girl's virtue is a predominant limerick theme. There are a number of such rhymes in this chapter, including a limerick about Myrtle snapping her legs shut like a turtle if tickled. Most limerick writers have the morals of an alley cat, if their work is any indication, and if I were Myrtle I would have done the same. Also in this chapter is a rare example of a limerick sequence that is actually funny. Producing a narrative poem using the limerick as the verse form is difficult, but this series about the man from Nantucket and his bucket is a winner.

There once was a gnu in a zoo
Who tired of the same daily view.
To seek a new sight
He stole out one night,
And where he went nobody gnew.

An eccentric old lady of Honiton,
(Whose conduct I once wrote a sonnet on)
Has now been in bed
With a cold in her head,
For a week with her boots and her bonnet on.

There was a fair maiden of Warwick
Who lived in the castle historic.
On the damp castle mould
She contracted a cold
And the doctor described paregarwick.

There was a young lady of Welwyn
Loved a barman who served in the Belwyn.
But the Belwyn, oh dear!
Had a welwyn the rear,
So they never wed for they felwyn.

~ ❧ ~

There once was an African Mau Mau
Got into a rather bad row-row.
The cause of the friction?
His practising diction,
Saying how-how now-now brown-brown cow-cow.

~ ❧ ~

There was a young lassie of Lancashire
Who landed a job as a bank cashier.
But she hardly knew
$1+1 = 2$
So had to give her place to another cashier.

The chief stewardess of a Boeing
When asked where the aircraft was going,
Said, "Our navigator
Is joining us later.
Until then we have no way of knowing."

A bather whose clothing was strewed
By winds, that left her quite nude
Saw a man come along
And, unless I am wrong,
You expected this line to be rude.

There was a young girl of Navarre
Who was frightfully fond of a tar.
When she followed him over
From Calais to Dover
Her friends cried, "That's going too far!"

There's a very mean man of Belsize
Who thinks he is clever and wise.
And, what do you think?
He saves gallons of ink,
By simply not dotting his i's!

There once was an artist called Lear
Who wrote verses to make children cheer.
Though they never made sense
Their success was immense
And the Queen thought Lear was a dear.

Who tarried in Jericho?
Until their beards did grow?
Judas Iscariot
Captain Marryat
And Harriet Martineau.

There was a young caddy from Powys
Who asked of his golfer, "Just howys
It possible for you
To perform as you do?"
Quoth he, "An amalgam of ability and prowys."

When you think of the hosts without no.
Who are slain by the giant cuco.
It's such a mistake
Of such food to partake
It results in a permanent slo.

An unpopular man of Cologne
With a pain in his stomach did mogne.
He heaved a great sigh
And said, "I would digh,
But the loss would be simply my ogne."

To an Irishman landing in heaven
Said St Peter, "We dine sharp at seven.
Then breakfast's at eight,
Never mind if you're late,
And there's Irish whiskey at eleven."

There was an old monk from Kilcrea,
Who of fasting grew tired every day.
Till at length with a yell,
He burst from his cell,
"From now on I'm going to be gay!"

There was an old lady from Mallow,
Whose complexion was just very tallow.
When asked for the cause
She replied without pause,
"Sure, three times a day I eat tallow."

These three limericks make a neat story.

There was an old man from Nantucket
Who kept all his cash in a bucket.
His daughter, called Nan,
Ran away with a man,
As for the bucket, Nantucket.

Pa followed the pair to Pawtucket
(The man and the girl with the bucket).
And he said to the man,
"You're welcome to Nan,"
But as for the bucket, Pawtucket.

Then the pair followed Pa to Manhasset,
Where he still held the cash as an asset,
And Nan and the man
Stole the money and ran,
And as for the bucket, Manhasset.

There was a young spinster of Ealing
Endowed with such delicate feeling
That she thought that a chair
Should not have its legs bare,
So she kept her eyes fixed on the ceiling.

There was an old lady of Harrow
Whose views were exceedingly narrow.
At the end of her paths,
She built two bird baths
For the different sexes of sparrow.

There was an old spinster of Fife
Who had never been kissed in her life.
Along came a cat
And she said, "I'll kiss that,"
But the cat meowed, "Not on your life!"

A lady from far Madagascar
Consented to marry a Lacsar.
Her friends thought 'twas naughty,
But she was past forty,
And he was the first man to ask her.

There was an old maid of Duluth
Who wept when she thought of her youth,
And the glorious chances
She'd missed at school dances
And once in a telephone booth.

A prudish old lady called Muir
Had a mind so incredibly pure
That she fainted away
At a friend's house one day
At the sight of a canary's manure.

The drawers of a spinster from Lavenham
Had rude limericks embroidered in Slav on 'em.
To her lawyer she said,
"Burn them all when I'm dead,
For I'm damned if my nephew is havin' 'em.

No one can tell about Myrtle
Whether she's sterile or fertile.
If anyone tries
To tickle her thighs
She closes them tight like a turtle.

A young lady sat on a quay,
Just as proper as proper can be.
A young fellow goosed her
But did not seduce her
So she thanked him and went home for tea.

A certain young woman named Terry
Got drunk on a small sip of sherry.
She'd insist upon games
With embarrassing names
Not in any refined dictionary.

There were once two people of taste
Who were beautiful down to the waist.
So they limited love
To the regions above
And thus remained perfectly chaste.

A prudish young girl of St Paul
Dreamt she undressed in the Mall.
The best of the joke
Was when she awoke
And found mud on her backside and all.

There was a young lady named Smith
Whose virtue was mostly a myth.
She said, "Try as I can,
I can't find a man
Who it's fun to be virtuous with."

While the prof wrote a Latin declension,
His pupils did things one can't mention.
Like shouting and shoving
Each other and showing
A singular lack of attention.

There was a young man of Bengal
Who went to a masquerade ball
Arrayed like a tree,
But he failed to foresee
His abuse by the dogs in the hall.

A maiden at college named Breeze
Weighed down by BAs and Litt Ds
Collapsed from the strain.
Alas, it was plain
She was killing herself by degrees.

Said a butcher's apprentice from Frome
Who aspired to be bride (and not groom),
"With some knives from the shop,
I shall do my own op."
And these words are inscribed on his tomb.

There was a young driver named Jake
Who made the most stupid mistake.
He drove through the wall
And into the hall
When he mixed up the gas and the brake.

There was a young fellow from Tyne
Put his head on the South-Eastern line.
But he died of ennui
For the five fifty-three
Didn't come till a quarter past nine.

A certain young gourmet of Crediton
Took some pâté de fois gras and spread it on
A chocolate biscuit,
Then murmured, "I'll risk it."
His tomb bears the date he said it on.

There was a schoolboy named Hannibal
Who won local fame as a cannibal
By eating his mother,
His father, his brother,
And his two sisters, Gertrude and Annabelle.

There was a young man from Laconia,
Whose mother-in-law had pneumonia.
    He hoped for the worst
    And after March the first
They buried her beneath a begonia.

There was a young joker named Tarr,
Who playfully pickled his ma.
    When he finished his work,
    He remarked with a smirk,
"This will make quite a family jar."

A farmer's daughter from Chigwell
Knew how to hoe and to dig well.
    When her father got ill,
    She grabbed up the swill
And fed all the tiniest pigs well.

I know an old lady called Meg
So hard-up she had to beg.
In one butcher's shop
She asked for a chop,
And pleaded for one chicken leg.

A man from Stockton-on-Tees
Produced phenomenal peas.
He then moved to Jarrow
And grew a green marrow
Too big to go in the deepfreeze.

There was a young man of Woking
Who didn't enjoy a soaking.
When told that real fellas
Don't use umbrellas
He said, "Why, you've got to be joking."

There was a man named Jason
Who trained to be a stonemason.
And one of his tips
Was "Catch all the chips
Then fry them in a deep basin."

I know a dry old stick
Whose wit is ready and quick.
He's been going to plays
Since Edwardian days
And calls himself "Very Old Vic."

A boy who can't stand the light
Only goes out when it is night.
He said to his dad,
"I know that you're sad
But everyone can't be so bright."

There was a young girl called Bella
Who loved life like a cave-dweller.
She travelled around
By the underground,
And owned her own flat in a cellar.

There was a young boy called Matt
Who lived with his mum in a flat.
When they moved to a house
They spotted a mouse,
So now they both live with a cat.

A naughty girl called Flo
Wanted her knickers to show.
She wore a skirt
As short as a shirt,
And kept on bending down low.

There was an old dame of Dunbar
Who took the 4:04 to Forfar.
But it went on to Dundee
So she travelled, you see,
Too far by 4:04 from Forfar.

A tutor who taught on the flute
Tried to teach two young tooters to toot.
Said the two to the tutor,
"Is it harder to toot, or
To tutor two tooters to toot?"

A young man called William S. Bugbee
Once said to a bedbug, "Don't bug me."
The bedbug told Bugbee,
"Please sit here and hug me,
'Cos I'm deathly afraid that you'll mug me."

If you catch a chinchilla in Chile
And then cut off its beard, willy-nilly,
  With a small razor blade,
  You can say that you've made
A Chilean chinchilla's chin chilly.

There was a young girl called Jill
Who said to Jack, "You're quite ill!
  It's quite absurd,
  Who ever heard
Of a well on top of a hill?"

A motorist called Sally
Didn't dilly-dally.
  She entered for fun,
  And finally won,
The Monte Carlo Rally.

A woman who wasn't too stunning
Competed in marathon running.
She really enjoys
Being chased by the boys.
Is she sporting or really quite cunning?

A Kentucky-bound author named Vaughan
Whose style often savoured of scorn,
Soon inscribed in his journals,
"Here the corn's full of kernels,
And the colonels are all full of corn."

There was a man in Atchison
Whose trousers had rough patches on.
He found them great
He'd often state
To strike his safety matches on.

A hen who resided in Reading
Attended a gentleman's wedding.
She walked up the aisle.
The guests had to smile
In spite of the tears they were shedding.

There was a young lady who said,
"Now remember, I want a good spread,
With puppy dogs' tails,
And plenty of snails,"
But she ended up sick in her bed.

There was an old lady of Crewe
Who made a thick, tasty stew
From toads and frogs,
She found in bogs.
But she just couldn't eat it, could you?

We brought cream cakes and a bun
For a picnic out in the sun.
She drank cups of tea,
From twelve until three
And never offered me one.

My greedy sister Nellie can
Make you believe she's a pelican.
It's not absurd,
For like that bird,
Her beak can hold more than her bellican.

A foul-mannered man, Mr Bustard
Liked to sweeten his tea with egg custard.
His conduct was gross,
He'd lick jam off his toast,
And his guests were truly disgusted.

There was a young girl called Dinah
Who wanted to marry a miner.
"I'll tell you why –
It's the gleam in his eye."
(But the lamp on his head is the shiner.)

There was a young lady from Cheam
Whose face caused her boyfriend to scream.
He'd kiss her in the dark
And, just for a lark,
He gave her some vanishing cream.

An ugly old man in Perth
Said he would give the earth
For a girl who replied
She would be his sweet bride –
Instead of dissolving in mirth.

There was a young man of Dumfries
Who had the most knobbly knees.
If he went to the park,
He'd go in the dark,
For dogs often mistook him for trees.

There was a young lady of Bandon
Whose feet were too narrow to stand on.
She stood on her head.
"For my motto,' she said,
"Has always been 'nil desperandum.'"

There was a young sailor named Bates
Who danced the fandango on skates.
But a fall on his cutlass
Rendered him nutless,
And practically useless on dates.

A buxom young typist named Baines
At her work took particular pains.
She was good at dictations
And long explanations,
But she ran more to bosom than brains.

There was a young woman of Glasgow,
Whose party proved quite a fiasco.
At 9:30 about
The lights all went out
Through a lapse on the part of the gas co.

There was a young person from Perth
Who was born on the day of his birth.
He was married, they say,
On his wife's wedding day,
And died when he quitted this earth.

Chapter 6

JOLLY FUNNY LIMERICKS

The limerick is essentially a humorous form. Many limericks are funny because they are a bit naughty, like the one about the girl from Tahiti. She is a bit flighty and owns a diaphanous nightie with which she titillates her neighbors. Others are funny because they are cruel, such as the one that starts with poor Ed being unable to sleep and ends with his head being stamped on. Zebedee losing his eyes in a fight and being unable to find the doctor to help him is in a similar vein.

There was a young man called Murray
Who tried to drive a big lorry.
He flattened a bus,
Which caused quite a fuss,
And he never even did say sorry.

A Frenchman named Jean-Pierre
Directed the Folies Bergère.
With a bit of greenery
And no other scenery
The stage looked curiously bare.

There was a young boy called Todd
Who wasn't a rocker or mod.
To his mum's great relief,
His only belief
Was that plaice was far better than cod.

All the guests at the animal fair
Had to dress up before they went there.
My friend Eddie Brian
Dressed up as a lion,
But I went in the nude, as a bear!

There was a young girl from St Paul
Wore a newspaper dress to a ball.
But the dress caught on fire
And burned her entire
Front page, sporting section and all.

A charming old lady of Settle
For a hat, wore a bright copper kettle.
When people derided,
She said, "I've decided
To show all the neighbours my mettle."

A thrifty young fellow of Shoreham
Made brown paper trousers and wore 'em.
He looked nice and neat
Till he bent in the street
To pick up a coin, then he tore 'em.

Said an eminent, erudite ermine,
"There's only one thing I cannot determine:
When a dame wears my coat
She's a person of note,
When I wear it I'm called only vermin."

There was once a lady of Erskine
Who had remarkably fair skin.
When I said to her, "Mabel,
You look well in sable,"
She replied, "I look best in my bearskin."

There was once a corpulent carp
Who wanted to play on the harp.
But to his chagrin,
So short was his skin,
He couldn't reach up to C sharp.

There once was a lady named Harris
That nothing seemed apt to embarrass.
Till the bath salts she shook
In the tub that she took
Turned out to be plaster of Paris.

A fat, lazy girl called Jill
Lived on a hill near Brill.
She'd sit on her trolley
And open her brolly
And let the wind blow her back up the hill.

The Latin poet Horace,
Said to his girlfriend Doris,
"Let Judas Iscariot
Have my chariot,
For I'm buying myself a new Morris."

A duel 'tween Regency rakes
May not have been for high stakes.
It's said that Lord Byron
Actually fired on
All but his closest of mates.

The famous astronomer Halley
Whose ambition was to dance ballet
Did a pas de deux
In a tutu of fur
When his comet was near to Spring Valley.

It is said that George the First
Screamed and ranted and cursed
Whenever his daughter
Spilled some of the water
She'd brought to slacken his thirst.

When Hitler was Germany's boss,
He never seemed at a loss
To decorate
A Nazi mate
With a ribbon and Iron Cross.

An arrogant child called Bart
Was just a little too smart.
His dad made him bend,
Then across his rear end
Bart learned what it felt like to smart.

A precocious girl from Devon
Fell in love from the age of seven.
When she gave up her toys
In favour of boys
She discovered that they were like heaven.

Said a salty old skipper of Wales,
"Number One, it's alright to chew nails.
It impresses the crew,
It impresses me too,
But stop spitting holes in the sails."

How remorselessly time seems to flow
Towards that brave dawn of two oh, oh, oh.
As I see the picture
The rich will get richer
And, oh yes, some computers will blow.

There was a young man of Devizes
Whose ears were of different sizes.
The one that was small
Was no use at all
But the other won several prizes.

There was a young gardener from Leeds
Who swallowed a packet of seeds.
In less than an hour
His nose was a flower,
And his head was a big bunch of weeds.

A man who came into some money
Decided to marry a bunny.
But the thought of the ears
And the tails of the dears
Made him skip it as being too funny.

There was an old fellow of Spain
Whose leg was removed by a train.
When his friends said, "How sad!"
He replied, "I'm glad,
For I've now lost my varicose veins."

A man who liked to philander,
Approached a young woman with candour.
All that she said,
Was, "Go and drop dead,"
Then struck him a mighty backhander.

There was a rich man named Sink.
To every young woman he'd wink,
And buy them things
Like diamonds and rings
And very expensive, rare mink.

A Victorian lady called Alice
Gave vent to her feelings of malice.
She thought that the Queen
Could be terribly mean,
And so she threw stones at the palace.

A man who enjoyed a bite
Insisted his food be just right.
He scarred the cook
With a butcher's hook
When his meat was too tough one night.

A Welshman known as Dai
Threw a custard pie
At Uncle Jack,
Who threw it right back
Right into Dai's right eye.

There was a young man called Dick
Who gave a hard kick to a brick.
Now what do you know,
Dick injured his toe,
And is hobbling around with a stick.

There was once a strong man named Russell
Who became involved in a tussle.
But he soon lost face
At a small seafood place,
When he struggled to open a mussel.

A captain yelled with great force,
"Oh where, oh where is my horse?"
His men looked around
But none could be found,
So the captain grew madder, of course.

A haughty young man playing chess
Made his moves with the utmost finesse.
But he pondered his fate
When his friend shouted, "Mate!
I've won, and I'm thankful, God Bless!"

There was a girl called Ada,
And did her mum upbraid her
For liking a bite
Right after midnight
And for being an icebox raider.

A bilious blighter from Bude
Was sloppy, greedy and rude.
He'd fill his tum,
Then ask his mum,
"Hey, Yo! Go get me some more food!"

An Italian, Valentino,
Whose appetite was obsceno
Filled his belly
With vermicelli
And several pints of red vino.

A famous grey mouse known as Micky
Was hungry and feeling quite picky.
He ate too much cheese
Then hollered, "Oh please
Get me a doctor, I feel sicky."

A poor, greedy man from Rye
Just loved to eat apple pie.
He sat on the floor
And ate forty-four
Which caused that poor man to die.

There was an old man of Calcutta
Who continually ate bread and butter
Till a big bit of muffin
On which he was stuffin'
Choked that old man of Calcutta.

There was a young girl called Daisy,
Not smart, but not at all crazy.
Did she work? Not at all,
She was what you might call
Just clever enough to be lazy.

A lazy young man called Norman
Had a job as a part-time doorman.
His only quirk
Was to shirk all work
And now Norman is a poor man.

There was a princess Amanda
Whose subjects just couldn't stand her.
She'd put up her feet
In the midsummer heat
Whilst servants stood over her and fanned her.

There is an old man named Duggie
Who rides everywhere in a buggy.
His feet just won't go
In rain or in snow
And his legs collapse if it grows muggy.

A soprano named Nancy McClee
Would sing for quite a large fee.
Why people would pay
To hear her each day
Is a mystery, she sings so off key.

I have a piano that's grand,
With music propped up on its stand.
But I feel that a cello,
Is really more mellow,
And I'd rather play that in a band.

There was a young lad called Mark
Who sang with the voice of a lark.
Then his throat got sore
And his tones grew poor
Now he sounds like a dog with a bark.

A production of the Mikado
Was presented in Colorado,
With Doris Day
And Faye Dunaway,
Who both sang with great bravado.

There was an old man from Hong Kong
Who wrote a peculiar song:
"Nothing could be finer,
Than to be in old Red China,"
Which he played on piano and gong.

Young boys who play on flutes
Are rarely hairy brutes.
But one fine day
Their sweet voices may
Deepen right down to their boots.

There was a flautist called Phil
Who, refusing to play even one trill,
Said, "I'll continue to play
When someone will pay
At least part of my bill."

Is it true that Robinson Crusoe
In time on his island grew so
Lonely and glum
That he started to hum
And finally sang like Caruso?

A lady musician called Anna
Took a working trip to Havana.
She played on the tuba
For the folks down in Cuba,
And dressed in a tropical manner.

There was a young lady of Ongar
Who specially liked dancing the conga.
It's really divine,
You dance in a line
Which quickly gets longer and longer.

A man who was learning the bassoon
Could hardly play it in tune.
When he got a note right
He'd play it all night
And through to the afternoon.

That young man, Zachariah,
Said he could sing, the liar.
Not one true note
Came out of his throat
So we threw him out of the choir.

A musical student named Carter
Was a truly magnificent farter.
On the strength of a bean
He'd fart *God Save the Queen*
And Beethoven's *Moonlight Sonata*.

I once knew a comic called Dawn
Whose jokes were as ripe as old corn.
She'd try to be punny
But just wasn't funny.
I wish that she'd never been born.

An unfortunate man called Zebedee
Was involved in a fight of some gravity.
When hit on the chin,
His eyeballs fell in
Now he can't even look for a remedy.

An elegant man from Soho
Had a very bad fall in the snow-ho.
With his dignity shaken
More care now he's takin',
He's careful but terribly slow-ho.

A young schizophrenic named Struther
When told of the death of his brother
Said, "Yes , it's too bad,
But I can't say it's sad,
After all, I still have each other."

A bear who only eats honey
(Preferring the thick to the runny)
Was bitten by bees
On all four of his knees,
Which he didn't find all that funny!

There was a young man called Ed
Who didn't sleep well on his bed.
He slumbered much more
Lying flat on the floor,
Till somebody stomped on his head.

Quicksands burp and bubble,
Better cross them at the double,
If not, you see,
You soon will be
Up to your neck in trouble.

At Christmas we visit Aunt Molly
Who's usually funny and jolly.
But last Boxing Day
Her temper gave way
When she fell in a pile of green holly.

There was a young model called Lola
Dressed in a black suit and a bowler.
With briefcase and brolly
She looked simply jolly,
Skating to work on one roller.

A Swiss man resembling a beaver
Lived under the lake in Geneva.
He swam and he swam
And installed by the dam
A sub-aqua TV receiver.

Said a man to his spouse in East Sydenham
"My best trousers! Now where have you hydenham?
It is perfectly true
They are not very new,
But I foolishly left half a quydenham."

There was a young maid in Tahiti
Whose neighbours considered quite flahiti
For if Monday was fine,
She'd hang on the line
An extremely diaphanous nahiti.

A young Irish servant in Drogheda
Had a mistress who often annogheda.
Whereon she would swear
With language so rare
That thereafter no one emplogheda.

There was a young fellow called Cholmondley
Who always, at dinner, sat dolmondly.
His fair partner said,
As he crumbled his bread,
"Dear me! You behave very rolmondely!"

There once was a boring young rev.
Who preached till it seemed he would nev.
His hearers en masse,
Got a pain in the ass
And prayed for relief of their neth.

There was a young lady of Munich
Whose appetite was simply unich.
　　She contentedly cooed
　　"There's nothing like food,"
As she let out a tuck in her tunich.

An ingenious girl named Brenda
Asked her friend Jane to lend her
　　A small paper clip
　　To hold up her slip
And a pin for the broken suspender.

A Welshman named Llewellyn
Dug a dungeon to dwell in,
　　But he forgot to dig stairs
　　And arrived unawares
In his cell – poor Llewellyn fell in.

A wise old prophet in Burma
Was frequently heard to murmur,
"Don't walk your dog
In marsh or bog.
Go where the ground is much firmer."

An unfortunate man, Stanley Hope,
Started to ski down a slope.
The slope was steep,
The snow was deep,
Did Stanley make it? Nope!

There was a young man of South Bray
Making fireworks one summer day.
He dropped his cigar,
In the gunpowder jar
There was a young man of South Bray.

A new servant girl named Maria
Had trouble lighting the fire
The wood being green,
She used gasoline,
Her position is now much higher.

There was a young man of Moose-Jaw
Who wanted to meet Bernard Shaw.
When they asked him, "Why?"
He made no reply,
But sharpened an axe and a saw.

There was a young lady of Malta
Who strangled her aunt with a halter.
She said, "I won't bury her;
She'll do for my terrier.
She'll keep for a month if I salt her."

A daring young fellow from Bangor
Sneaked a super-swift jet from its hangar.
When he crashed in the bay,
Neighbours led him away
In rather more sorrow than anger.

There was a young fellow called Clyde
Who once at a funeral was spied.
When asked who was dead,
He smilingly said:
"I don't know, I just came for the ride."

Said a gleeful young man from Torbay,
"This is really a red-letter day,
For I've poisoned with sherbet
My rich Uncle Herbert
Because he had too much to say."

There was a young lady of Spain
Who was terribly sick on a train.
Not once, but again,
And again and again,
And again and again and again.

There was an old lady of Tooting
Who wanted to learn parachuting.
Though they tried to repress her
She jumped from the dresser,
A perfect fall executing.

The bishop of Ebu Plantation
Wrote a thesis on transfiguration
For the *Christian Review*
(As all good bishops do)
While practising miscegenation.

There was a young maid who said, "Why
Can't I look in my ear with my eye?
If I gave my mind to it
I'm sure I can do it,
You never can tell till you try."

There was a young lady named Bunny
Whose kisses were sweeter than honey.
Her callers galore
Would line up at her door
To take turns in paying her money.

There was a young lady named Cager
Who, as a result of a wager,
Consented to fart
The whole oboe part
Of Mozart's Quartet in F major.

There once was a monk of Camyre
Who was seized with a carnal desire.
And the primary cause
Was the Abbess's drawers
Which were hung up to dry by the fire.

There was a young girl of Cape Cod
Who thought babies were fashioned by God.
But 'twas not the Almighty
Who hiked up her nightie –
'Twas Roger the lodger, by God!

A hot-tempered girl of Caracas
Was wed to a samba-mad jackass.
When he started to cheat her
With a dark señorita
She kicked him right in the maracas.

Chapter 7

THE FUNNIEST LIMERICKS EVER

Limericks can, amongst many of their attributes, be surreal. Lear's nonsense verses are surreal and charming; other, more modern verses, while not displaying the imaginative nonsense of the "poet laureate of the limerick," still make their protagonists jump through some fairly improbable hoops. As an example, there is Kate, who, for a rest, sat on a farmer's gate. The bull, who must have had personal problems, threw her into the air where she stayed until eight. I suppose that if he threw her into the air at 7:59.59 the limerick is only reflecting reality, though I imagine we are expected to believe that she was thrown around tea time. Poor Kate.

On a hot summer's day on his bicycle,
Lenny peddles while eating an icicle.
If he loses his grip
He'll start to slip,
And he'll wish he still had his tricycle.

I was bad at speaking and gramma
So I took up throwing the hamma.
I hit my own head
And now I'm in bed
And I can't even stutta or stamma.

I have an Auntie Mo
Who's really quite whacko.
She took a gun
To shoot her son
But missed, and hit her toe.

A swimmer in the Adriatic
Was floating about, quite static.
But when he saw
A fin and a jaw,
His movements became quite dramatic.

There was an anthologist who
Decided that nothing's taboo.
Her words are so rude
Her verses so lewd,
I'm sure they'll appeal to you.

Well it's partly the shape of the thing
That gives the old limerick wing.
Those accordion pleats
Full of airy conceits
Take it up like a kite on a string.

There was a young poet from Milan
Who wrote verses no one could scan.
When he was asked why,
He would always reply,
"Because I always want to make the last line
as long as I can."

A fruiterer from Blandford Forum
Used a sharp knife on apples to core 'em.
The knife sliced his skin
So remarkably thin
That the flesh left formed more than a quorum.

There was a young lady of Riga
Who smiled as she rode on a tiger.
They returned from the ride
With the lady inside
And a smile on the face of the tiger.

There was once an orthodox preacher
Who fancied himself a great teacher.
His was a technique
Negative and oblique
To scare the hell from every creature.

There was a young man from Darjeeling
Who boarded a bus bound for Ealing
The note on the door
Said don't spit on the floor,
So he carefully spat on the ceiling.

There was a young boy called Jim
Who fractured his right lower limb.
He leapt in a pool
Without water, the fool.
Good heavens! He must have been dim.

My friend, who comes from Stanmore,
Fell asleep by the baking seashore.
Her eyebrows were fried,
She was burnt on each side,
And her cheeks are painfully sore.

A foolish young girl called Kate
Sat down on a farmer's gate.
A bull, in despair,
Threw her high in the air
And she didn't come down until eight.

There was an old man from Penzance
Who always wore cast-iron pants.
He said, "Some years back,
I sat on a tack
And I'll never again take that chance."

A hard-hearted boy named Neil
Claimed he didn't know how to feel.
But when I put some ants
Down the back of his pants,
He suddenly learnt how to squeal.

There was an old man from Dunoon
Who set out on a trip by balloon.
The man came off worst
When the big balloon burst,
And he landed back home rather soon.

There was a young man called Dale
Who wanted to eat a whale.
He mashed it with cheese
And served it with peas,
But couldn't quite manage the tail.

There was a strange fellow called Matt
Who wanted to look like a cat.
His feet were like paws,
With retractable claws,
And whiskers grew out of his hat.

A venturesome three-week old chamois
Strayed off in the wood from his mamois,
And might have been dead
But some picnickers fed
Him with sandwiches, milk and salamois.

There was a young man from the city
Who met what he thought was a kitty.
He gave it a pat
And said, "Nice little cat."
They buried his clothes, out of pity.

The bashful young bachelor Cleary
Of girls was exceedingly leary.
Then a lady named Lou
Showed him how and with who
He could render his evenings more cheery.

A certain old maid in Cohoes
In despair taught her bird to propose.
But the parrot, dejected
At being accepted,
Spoke some lines to profane to disclose.

An unpopular youth of Cologne
With a pain in his stomach did mogne.
He heaved a great sigh,
And said, "I wish I could digh,
But the loss would be only my ogne."

A señora who strolled on the Corso
Displayed quite a lot of her torso.
A crowd soon collected
And no one objected,
Though some were in favour of more so.

～⁂～

A fanatic gun-lover named Crust
Was perverse to the point of disgust.
His idea of a peach
Had a sixteen-inch breech
And a pear-handled .44 bust.

～⁂～

A team playing baseball in Dallas
Called the umpire names out of malice.
While that worthy had fits
The team made eight hits
And a girl in the bleachers named Alice.

There once was a daring park warden,
Who thought as he lay in his garden,
"It's not really rude
To be caught in the nude,
As long as I mutter, 'Beg Pardon.'"

There was a young man called Vince
Who made his poor barber wince.
He used the leg of a chair
To comb through his hair
Then demanded to have a pink rinse.

There was a young lady of Slough
Who claimed she didn't know how
To quack like a duck,
Though she tried without luck,
But boy she knew how to meow.

There was a young man from Quebec
Who wrapped both legs round his neck.
But then he forgot
How to untie the knot,
And now he's an absolute wreck.

A timid young man when a tot
Fell into a giant teapot.
But as he grew older,
That man grew bolder
And flew out of the spout like a shot.

There was a young girl called Anna
Who had a superior manner.
She drove fast cars
To cocktail bars,
And puffed on a mammoth Havana.

A businessman called Señor Prado
Tried to buy the state of Colorado.
Some doctors from Spain
Examined his brain
And discovered it filled with bravado.

There was an old man of Neath
Who drilled holes in all his front teeth.
When he drank water
He'd squirt his young daughter
'Cause water would spurt through his teeth.

There once was a kind-hearted king
Who taught a poor chicken to sing
By using his crown
To bang, till sundown,
On a kettle tied up with string.

A young man who had chosen
To go to sea as a bosun
Is in a poor way
Just north of Norway
With all of his assets frozen.

There is an old man in York
Who draws on the pavement in chalk.
He makes a few pence,
But he gets very tense
When over his work people walk.

The fabulous wizard of Oz
Retired from the business because
What with up-to-date science,
To most of his clients
He wasn't the wizard he was.

A policeman pounding the beat
Must never rest on a seat.
He must persevere,
And keep walking, I fear,
Even with two aching feet.

There was a Welsh dentist called Keith
Whose practice was well known in Neath.
He made himself ill
Perfecting his skill
Extracting all his own teeth.

Young farmers have to learn
That chickens can be quite stern.
If you grab their eggs
From between their legs
They'll bite your bum in return.

I know of a man who's a Quaker,
He works dawn to dusk as a baker.
But one day by mistake
He was cooked with a cake,
And now he's meeting his maker.

You know that a pig is a hog,
And can tell a cat from a dog.
But it's perfectly true
That all of them do
Look exactly the same in the fog.

We know that furry white rabbits
Breed quickly – it's one of their habits.
They canoodle all day,
Hop, skip and play,
That's life for nature's own rabbits.

There was an old man of Whitehaven
Whose whiskers had never been shaven.
He said, "It is best,
For they make a nice nest
In which I can keep my pet raven."

A cat in the town of St Ives
Stole honey from several large hives.
Once stung by eight bees,
He said, "Stop it please!
You know I have only nine lives."

We have an intelligent cat
Who refuses to hunt mouse or rat.
She'll lie and wait
For food on her plate,
Now who can blame her for that?

There once was a man with two poodles
Whose names were Toodles and Doodles.
Their favourite dish
Was not made of fish —
The poodles loved oodles of noodles.

There was a female antelope
Who loved a big male antelope.
But he banged his knee
Against an oak tree,
And now they can't elope.

In the zoo there's an animal, Hamel,
A spitting young ornery camel.
He's rather be free,
Like a bird or a bee,
And hates being classified "mammal."

Though big, a hippopotamus
Is very clearly not a bus,
Although at the zoo
For a quid or two
He gave a ride to a lot of us.

This gull is called a kittiwake,
And people near the shore awake
To feed this bird,
When winds are heard,
With bread and bits of gritty cake.

There once was a bald gorilla
Who, wrapped up in a furry chinchilla,
Escaped from the zoo
Through a gap in the loo,
And now works in a café in Manila.

A certain young lady of Slough
Is widely considered a cow.
Her name is Mary,
She's down at the dairy
Along with the hen and the sow.

A curious bird is the bunting,
You'll hear it if you go hunting.
It has an odd cry
That sounds like a sigh
And a railway engine shunting.

A curious bird is the crow,
The blackest fowl I know.
It is out of sight
In the middle of the night,
But how does it hide in the snow?

A curious bird is the gull
Which lives on the isle of Mull.
Just on a hunch,
It flew out to lunch
On some fish in faraway Hull.

A wonderful bird is the toucan,
It eats just as much as you can.
Is it able to speak
With food in its beak?
It's said that the one in the zoo can.

An optimistic young man named Ted
Was born with a hole in his head.
Good job it's not two,
Or the wind blowing through
Would make it terribly draughty.

I'm bored to death by Harrison,
His jokes and puns are embarrassing.
But I quite like the bum,
He's as dumb as they come,
Which makes me feel bright by comparison.

A cheerful old bear at the zoo
Could always find something to do.
If it bored him to go
On a walk to and fro,
He'd turn round and walk fro and to.

There was a young lady of Leeds
Who planted an assortment of seeds.
The birds pecked up most,
But still she can boast
Of a rose and a garden of weeds.

There was a young wife from Uganda,
Renowned for her coolness and candour.
When, during abuse,
Someone said, "You goose!"
She quickly retorted, "Uganda!"

There was a young girl called Joni
Who ate plates of boiled macaroni.
She got very fat,
But she didn't mind that
'Cos she bounced when she fell off her pony.

There was a young man called Shane
Who had a very small brain.
He wasn't too bright
But that was all right,
'Cos headaches caused him no pain.

There was a young girl called Harris
Whom doctors were wont to embarrass.
If one came to her bed
She'd blush a bright red,
Even in plaster of Paris.

There was a young man from Dumbarton
Who thought he could run like a Spartan.
On the thirty-ninth lap
His braces went snap,
And his face went a red patterned tartan.

There was a young bather from Bewes
Who lay on the bank of the Ouse.
His radio blared
And passers-by stared,
For all he had on was the news.

A young belly dancer from Hythe
Was extremely supple and lithe.
When a naughty spider
Crept somewhere inside her,
Oh did she wriggle and writhe.

There once was a ghost called Paul,
Who went to a fancy-dress ball.
To shock all the guests
He went quite undressed
But the rest couldn't see him at all.

A pretty young girl called Jean
Jumped high on the trampoline.
The boys laughed in roars
At the sight of her drawers,
The first bloomers they'd ever seen.

There was a young lady of Tottenham,
Her manners – she'd wholly forgotten 'em.
Whilst at tea at the Vicar's
She took off her knickers,
Explaining she felt much too hot in 'em.

A lady of limited means
Lives only on peas and baked beans.
She doesn't have furs
And her clothes aren't hers,
Which leads to embarrassing scenes.

All the audience views
Of the readers on the *Nine O'Clock News*
Is the smart upper half,
But it might prove a laugh
If we saw all the way to their shoes.

There was a young man of Kuwait
Who was late and just couldn't wait.
He complained to the waiter,
Who said, "I'll come later
To wait on you so you must wait."

There's a place in Wales called the Mumbles
That is filled with groans and grumbles.
The locals complain
Of constant cold rain,
Which produces a coastline that crumbles.

My cousin is a high-class lawyer
Who's so snobbish he's likely to ignore yer.
If he starts to speak,
As he did last week,
He's most certainly going to bore yer.

A teacher from Leamington Spa
Said to her Pa and her Ma,
"A boy whom I taught
Is a brave astronaut –
I said that one day he'd go far!"

The modern delivery man
Arrives in a very smart van.
But some years ago,
As we old ones know,
The errand boys all simply ran.

Chapter 8

～✤～

A LIMERICK LUCKY DIP

This chapter contains a general selection of limericks that do not otherwise have a home to go to. A number depend for their humor on the pronunciation of old English names, which, to confuse the uninitiated and foreigners, are not pronounced as they are spelt. In one, Beauchamp rhymes with teach 'em; in another, Alnwick rhymes with Titanic, which just goes to show how inventive limericks can get. Others rely not on celebrating the idiosyncracies of the British class system but in making fools of the pompous. The limerick about a chap called Ddodd insisting on his four "ds" when God is happy with one is a good example.

There was a strong man in Russia
Whose flat could not have been plusher.
Girls came to his place,
But found his embrace
Was more like a giant car crusher.

Once out on the lake at Dubuque
A girl took a row with a duque.
He remarked, "I am sure,
You are honest and pure,"
Then leaned right over to puque.

A small boy who lived in Iquique
Had a voice annoyingly squiquie.
When his father said, "Oil it,
My son, or you'll spoil it,"
His retort was a trifle too chique.

In a bus queue bound for Kew
Thus was hailed by a Scot, who he knew.
"Dinna fash yersel, Lew,
I'm paying for you!"
And the few who o'erheard, whistled, "phew!"

An obstinate lady of Leicester
Wouldn't marry her swain, though he preicester.
For his income I fear
Was a hundred a year,
On which he could never have dreceister.

She frowned and called him "Mr"
Because in sport he kr.
And so in spite,
That very night,
That Mr kr sr.

There was a mechalnwick of Alnwick
Whose opinions were very Germalnwick.
So when war had begun
He went off with a gun
The proportions of which were Titalnwick.

A youthful schoolmistress of Beauchamp
Said, "These awful boys, how shall I teauchamp?
For they will not behave,
Although I look grave
And with tears in my eyes I beseauchamp."

There was a young fellow named Fisher
Who was fishing for fish in a fissure.
Then a cod, with a grin,
Pulled the fisherman in.
Now they're searching the fissure for Fisher.

A sensitive girl called O'Neill
Went on the fairground big wheel.
When halfway round
She looked down at the ground –
It cost her a two-dollar meal.

There was a young fellow named Cass
Whose bollocks were made out of brass.
When they tinkled together
They played Stormy Weather,
And lightning shot out of his ass.

A book and a jug and a dame
And a nice cozy nook for there same.
"And I don't care a damn,"
Said Omar Khayyam,
"What you say, it's a great little game."

An assistant professor named Ddodd
Had manners arresting and odd.
He replied, "If you please,
Spell my name with four 'd's."
Though one was was sufficient for God.

~·⟨∘⟩·~

There was a young lady of Dee
Went to bed with each man she could see.
When it came to a test
She wished to be best,
And practice makes perfect, you see.

~·⟨∘⟩·~

There was a young lady of Eton
Whose figure had plenty of meat on.
She said, "Marry me, dear,
And you'll find that my rear
Is a nice place to warm your cold feet on."

There was a young lady named Etta
Who fancied herself in a sweater.
Three reasons she had,
To keep warm was not so bad,
But the other two reasons were better.

In summer she said she was fair,
In autumn her charms were still there.
But he said to his wife
In the winter of life,
"There's no spring in your old derrière."

A stripteaser up in Fall River
Caused a sensitive person to quiver.
The aesthetic vibration
Brought soulful elation,
Besides, it was good for the liver.

A reckless young man from Fort Blainey
Made love to a spinster named Janie.
When his friends said, "Oh dear,
She's so old and so queer,"
He replied, "But the day was so rainy."

There was a young girl whose frigidity
Approached cataleptic rigidity,
Till you gave her a drink,
When she quickly would sink
In a state of complaisant liquidity.

A lady from way down in Ga
Became quite a notable fa.
But she faded from view
With a quaint IOU
Then she signed, "Miss Lucrezia Ba."

There once lived a certain Miss Gale
Who turned most impressively pale,
For a mouse climbed her leg
(Don't repeat this I beg)
And a splinter got caught in its tail.

There was a young maiden named Hoople
Whose bosom was triple, not douple.
So she had one removed
But it grew back improved
And at present her front is quadruple.

There was a young person of Jaipur
Who fell madly in love with a viper.
With screams of delight
He'd retire each night
With the viper concealed in a diaper.

There was a great lord in Japan
Whose name on a Tuesday began.
It carried through Sunday
Till twilight on Monday,
And sounded like stones in a can.

There was a young lady called Kate
Who necked in the dark with her date.
When asked how she fared,
She said she was scared,
But otherwise doing first-rate.

There was a young lady of Kent
Who said she knew what it meant
When men asked her to dine,
Gave her cocktails and wine.
She knew what it meant but she went.

A pansy who lived in Khartoum
Took a lesbian up to his room.
And they argued a lot
About who should do what
And how and with which and to whom.

There was an old girl of Kilkenny,
Whose usual charge was a penny.
For half that sum,
You might fondle her bum,
A source of amusement to many.

A corpulent lady named Kroll
Had an idea exceptionally droll.
She went to a ball
Dressed in nothing at all
And backed in as a Parker House roll.

There was a young girl who would make
Advances to snake after snake.
She said, "I'm not vicious,
But so superstitious!
I do it for grandmother's sake."

If you find for your verse there's no call,
And you can't afford paper at all,
For the poet true born,
However forlorn,
There's always the lavatory wall.

A conceited young boy called Rob
Was commonly known as a snob.
When asked to make tea,
He'd say, "No, not me,
That certainly isn't my job."

There was a young lady of Slough
Who said that she didn't know how.
Till a young fellow caught her
And jolly well taught her,
And she lodges in Pimlico now.

There was a young lady of Florence
Who for kissing professed great abhorrence.
But when she'd been kissed
And found what she missed,
She wept till the tears came in torrents.

There was a young man from Toledo
Who travelled about incognito.
The reason he did
Was to bolster his id
Whilst pleasing his huge, massive ego.

Have you heard of the boxer named Jules
Whose appetite for food never cools?
He pays no attention
To social convention
Or the Marquess of Queensbury's rules.

There once was a Roman, Ignatius,
Who met a man called Horatius.
Said Ig, "Our names
Both end the same,"
Said Horace, "So they do, good gracious."

There was a young girl called Clarisse
Who liked to be called Miss Harris.
Or "Sweet Mam'selle"
Would please her quite well
If she ever travelled to Paris.

A runner from New Orleans
Lives entirely on fresh greens.
He moves with great speed,
And stays in the lead,
Because he's stuffed with runner beans.

A one-legged man in a kilt
Had a special appliance built.
In Aberdeen
He can be seen
On a crutch and a tall wooden stilt.

There was a young woman called Sue
Who saw a strange beast in a zoo.
When she asked, "Is it old?"
She was firmly told,
"No, certainly not, it's a gnu."

There was a young lady of Zion
Looked round for a shoulder to cry on.
So she married a spouse
From a very old house
And started to cry on the scion.

Cried a slender young lady called Toni,
With a bottom exceedingly bony,
"I'll say this for my rump:
Though it may not be plump
It's my own, not a silicone phoney."

I sat next to the justice at tea.
It was just as I feared it would be.
Her rumblings abdominal
Were simply phenomenal,
And everyone thought it was me.

There was a naughty old friar
Who had to report to the prior.
The prior told Tuck,
"You've run out of luck,
I've just seen you smoking your briar."

An acrobat called Uriah
Could cartwheel and jump even higher.
He'd put on wet clothes,
Spin round on his toes,
The very first tumble dryer.

A businessman named Shore
Owned a jewellery store.
The goods he sold
Were rings of gold,
I'm sure Shore wasn't poor.

An artist named Botticelli
Painted a model named Nellie.
She slapped him, "Take that!
You've painted me fat,
I'm slim and I've been on the telly."

The author Thomas Hardy
Was ever so lardi-dar-di.
He'd say, if late
For a scheduled debate,
"Forgive me for being so tardy."

The famous composer Liszt,
Was enraged and brought down his fist
On the piano keys
So hard that he's
Just broken a bone in his wrist.

The composer Benjamin Britten
Owned a musical kitten.
It played lovely tunes
On piano and spoons
Much better than Britten had written.

A certain young lady named Lily
Likes knickers – light pink and frilly.
In winter she wears
Maybe three or four pairs,
To keep her from feeling too chilly.

An eccentric old man named Bill
Lived in a cottage in Dill.
He dried his socks
In the window box
And his underwear on the sill.

A golfer who came from Calcutta
Had thoughts much too pungent to utter
When his wife, as he found
Ere commencing a round,
Was whisking the eggs with his putter.

There was a young lady of Dee
Who went down to the river to swim.
A man in a punt
Stuck an oar in his eye
And now she wears glasses you see.

The devil who plays a deep part
Has tricked his way into your heart
By simple insistence
On his non-existence,
Which really is devilish smart.